EMBRACING
THE RACE

EMBRACING THE RACE

40 Devotions for the Runner's Soul

LISA PREUETT

CROSSLINK
PUBLISHING

Embracing The Race: 40 Devotions for the Runner's Soul

CrossLink Publishing
www.crosslinkpublishing.com

ISBN 978-1-63357-072-6

Library of Congress Control Number: 2016934815

ACKNOWLEDGMENTS

I give all the glory and honor for this book to my Lord and Savior Jesus Christ. He is the one who opens my eyes to the powerful parallels between running and our journey of faith.

My amazing husband, Jim. You're my biggest cheerleader in my passion for running. Thanks for bearing with me on those countless mornings I'd rise early for a run, waking you from much needed sleep. I'll cherish the moments you've greeted me at the finish line with a bouquet of flowers.

My children, Aaron and Breanna. Thanks for your patience with me in my running journey, especially when I collapsed on the couch after many long runs. As long as I have breath in my lungs, I'll pray for you both to embrace the life God's given you.

Kim Pryor, without your encouragement I never would've believed I could run any distance farther than a 5K. Your supportive words and passion for running inspired me to keep going.

My Southeast Christian Church running group. The motivation, encouragement, and inspiration you've given to me, and many others, is such a huge blessing. Without this group, my running journey would have come to a dead end.

I'm also blessed with a multitude of family and friends who've encouraged me to pursue my writing dreams!

TABLE OF CONTENTS

INTRODUCTION

If you're assuming the author of this devotional book for runners is a natural athlete—born to run—then you'd be mistaken. The truth is I absolutely used to *hate* running. Not one ounce of athleticism in my bones, I was one of the last kids picked for sports teams in school gym classes. *Not her; pick someone else!* The only sport I ever played was youth softball. But because it was a church league, they really couldn't turn anyone away. This was more about hanging out with friends and having fun. The only running required was the short distance in between bases—but that was only if you actually *hit the ball.* So, I really didn't have to worry about running very much!

As a sophomore in high school gym class, I dreaded the week we had to run *one* mile around the track. This was a required task. Either complete it or get a failing grade. My *only* motivation was to fulfill the requirement. I couldn't let this ruin my GPA and honor roll status.

I came down with a horrible cold the day before the assigned mile run. Home in bed, I desperately hoped I wouldn't have to make up the missed run. My hope vanished when my gym teacher informed me I *did* have to make it up—on my own time after school! Those four laps around the track felt like an eternity. My slow jogging turned into a sluggish stroll with each step. Gasping for air, I felt like I would surely pass out. Stopwatch in hand, my teacher waited on the sideline. She probably hoped I'd hurry up so she could go home. Full of misery, I trudged around the track one last time. Handing me a cup of water, my teacher declared, "You finally did it. You're done for this grading period."

You bet I was done! I resolved that day I would *never* run again. Running was pure misery—no fun at all. I just wanted to go home and collapse. What I didn't know *then* was that I didn't enjoy running in that moment because it was something I *had* to do.

In the years that followed, I faithfully kept my vow to never run. I graduated college, got married, had a couple of kids. Life was good. But at age forty-two, I realized my metabolism wasn't what it used to be. I wasn't overweight, but I felt sluggish and wanted to get in shape (just enough to maintain my weight and still eat junk food when I wanted). My husband and I joined a fitness center. I enjoyed working out, toning my muscles, and lifting weights. I even stepped on the treadmill for fast *walks*. But the elliptical machine became my best friend—a great cardio booster, but it wasn't *running*.

A short time later, I was inspired by my brother, Jeff, when he registered to run a half marathon. He and his wife were in the process of adopting their daughter from Ethiopia. He invited friends and family to make donations, helping them raise money for the adoption fees. Twenty-plus years had passed since he'd run this same race in high school, but here he was—running for a cause. With a *purpose*.

Just weeks later, I heard about an upcoming 5K race in the rural county where I live. *Could I do it?* I was in great shape. Maybe now I could actually *run*. If my brother could run thirteen miles after all those years, surely I could run a simple 5K. Yes, I was about to break my twenty-seven-year vow of no running.

Stepping onto level pavement in my neighborhood, excitement—and not dread—flowed through my veins. Starting with a slow jog, I breathed in the air with determination. My first goal was a half mile. Although slow, I found my pace—never stopping to walk. Over the next several weeks I gradually ran longer distances until I finally reached three miles. I'd found my comfortable pace, thankful my neighborhood roads were smooth. No intense hills or uneven sidewalks. Running this course repeatedly, I figured I was ready for race day.

Following directions for the race location, I parked my car in a field next to a heavily wooded area. Nervously looking for the start line, I asked someone where to go. "Oh, the cross country course starts over there and runs all through the trails." *What did he say? Where was the paved road I'd envisioned?* Runners made their way to the start line—facing the edge of the woods. The excitement for running my first 5K turned to embarrassment. This was *not* what I signed up for! My original goal was to run the race without stopping. Now I wondered if I'd even finish. I'd come this far and couldn't back down. My family was there to support me. I couldn't let them down. *I'll do this and check it off my bucket list.*

Just seconds into the race, I brushed past tree limbs and almost tripped over roots on the narrow trail. People passed me quickly, almost knocking me down. Looking ahead, I noticed—and felt—a steep incline. I'd never run uphill before. My slow jog fizzled out quickly. Catching my breath, I had to walk. The path continued to twist and turn, and suddenly my feet stepped into a pile of horse manure! Why didn't someone clean this up before the race? Stepping off the trail, I attempted to wipe my shoes off. I desperately prayed, *"God, this isn't what I signed up for; please get me through this!"*

Back on the trail, I kept going. More twists, turns, uphill, downhill, tripping over roots—this was no fun. Why hadn't I checked into this 5K more thoroughly? If I'd known this was a *trail run*, I never would have done it. I'd trained for a month. All that time and effort—for this? Trudging up the final hill, I heard people cheering. The finish line must be close; I couldn't wait to be done. My short-lived excitement for running had almost disappeared. But that's when I heard it—the gentle voice of God whispering to my weary heart.

Lisa, this race is a lot like your walk with me. You want to figure out life according to your expectations. But that's not how I created life to be. You aren't in charge of your course. I am. You need to trust me through the twists, turns, hills and obstacles. I'll even be with you when life gets messy. Keep on running; there's more I want you to discover.

I finished my first 5K and it wasn't my last. The way I heard God speak to my soul that day was *profound*. Running became a major part of my life from that day forward. With the support of a running group, I've run multiple 5K's, 10K's, half-marathons, a full marathon, and (gulp!) even a Tough Mudder. My faith has grown by leaps and bounds! While God speaks to me in other ways, I usually hear Him speak most clearly when I'm running.

And so this book is an overflow of what God has shown me. They are reflections from a runner's perspective. But even if you've never run a day in your life, you'll still gain wisdom and insight. In the New Testament, the apostle Paul writes about our walk of faith being just like a race. So no matter where you are in your race, I pray you'll embrace it and be encouraged as you read the pages ahead.

In Christ,
Lisa

NO TURNING BACK

John 14:6 "I am the way, the truth and the life. No one comes to the Father except through me."

"You mean you're going to pay money to run?"

Yes, this is the question many people ask when you mention you've just registered for your first race. For those who've never run, it really doesn't make sense that someone would actually pay money to do something that seems so exhausting. It's one thing to *talk* about signing up for a race, it's another to actually go online, register, give your credit card information, and finally click the submit button. Once you've clicked that button, it's a done deal. You're in. No turning back.

The first time I registered for a race, I wavered back and forth. *Do I really want to do this? Do I have enough time to train for this race? What if something comes up and I can't make it? Am I really cut out for this?* But once I clicked the submit button, I knew I'd made a commitment. I was all in. There is no *maybe* option when you register for a race. You either do it or you don't. Once you've made the commitment, there's an immediate urgency to follow through with the necessary training. You've paid a price and you don't want to lose your investment. *Now that I've signed up, what's the next step?*

Is this how we approached the crossroad when we decided to become a follower of Christ? Did we really ponder what we were signing up for? Did we consider the cost? Did we truly realize the commitment we were making when we said *yes* to him? Was there an urgency to follow through with the next step?

The good news is that when you give your life to Christ, you don't have to pay anything. No fees. No credit card number required. In this case, he's the one who paid the price up front. He's the one who gave freely of himself. He did this while we were still sinners, knowing that many of those he died for might choose to reject the option of signing up for the race. Yet he still did it. For everyone. For me. For you.

Although it doesn't cost you anything tangible, there's still a cost. There's an investment we make. We don't have to do anything to earn salvation; we're saved by faith and grace. But it will cost us something when we come out of our comfort zone. It will cost us our pride, selfishness, and desire to take control of our life. When we say *yes* to Jesus, it means we say *no* to the ways of this world while allowing him to live out his purpose through us. When we signed up to run the race of faith, we clicked the *submit* button. We chose to fully surrender and *submit* to him .

What we get in return is of much more value than anything this world has to offer. Dear friend, we receive eternal life! Forgiveness of our sins. Overflowing joy. Peace and hope for our weary souls. You can't assign a value to what we receive when we sign up to run this race. It doesn't compare to anything. It's priceless.

READY? If you call yourself a follower of Christ, are you all in? When you first came to him, did you consider what it would cost you? Did you consider what it cost *him*? Are you living your life fully committed to him? What is your next step?

GET SET. Luke 14:27–28 "And anyone who does not carry his cross and follow me cannot be my disciple. Suppose one of you wants to build a tower. Will he not first sit down and estimate the cost to see if he has enough money to complete it?"

GO! *Jesus, I praise you for what you've done for me on the cross. Thank you for the gift of salvation. Thank you for the promise of eternal life. Help me to live each day with a heart fully devoted to you as I continue with the commitment I've made to be your follower. Amen.*

ARE YOU THOROUGHLY EQUIPPED?

2 Timothy 3:16–17 "All scripture is God-breathed and is useful for teaching, rebuking, correcting and training in righteousness, so that the servant of God may be thoroughly equipped for every good work."

If you've lived in the runner's world for any length of time, you're familiar with all the specialty stores lined with endless racks of nothing but running attire: shoes, socks, shorts, shirts, jackets, and hats. These items are pricy, yet each piece is essential if you desire to be thoroughly equipped for running your race effectively.

I shook my head in disbelief when I paid $120 for my first pair of running shoes. *Really? Why can't I just wear the cute tennis shoes I got on sale at Target?* A friend of mine—an experienced marathon runner—explained the facts to me about running shoes: "If you don't have the proper shoes, you'll be miserable." I had to experience aching feet and knee pain before I realized I didn't have the right shoes. Shoes are to a runner what tires are to a car. Attempting to use the wrong type is damaging and utterly reckless.

It's essential to equip yourself with uniquely-designed socks allowing your feet to breathe and avoid blisters. There's a myriad of shorts, shirts, and jackets specially designed for every season of weather.

God also calls us to be thoroughly equipped. If we're going to run our race of faith well, we've got to be prepared. What does he call us to equip ourselves with? According to today's key verse (2 Timothy 3:16—17), he's speaking about the *word of God*. We must equip ourselves with the powerful words from scripture. These powerful words must enter through our mind and then penetrate like deep roots to the depth of our soul. We have to intentionally embrace them, meditate on them, ponder them continually, and digest them through every fiber of our heart. In doing so we will be prepared for every situation we face.

The scripture in Timothy tells us God's word will teach us. So we must embrace it and allow our hearts to soak up the knowledge of who he is and how he desires for us to live. His word will also rebuke and correct us when we stumble and get off course. These moments may be difficult, yet we're promised his truth will set us free. God's word also trains us for the purposes he's called us to. The power of his word enables us to humbly walk in the righteousness of Christ. (2 Timothy 3:16-17)

Just as we invest in essential running attire, Christ followers must make an investment. Not with money—but with our time and effort. We must be intentional with prioritizing our lives around God's word, no matter what the cost may be. I foolishly thought the cheap tennis shoes were sufficient, yet I suffered the consequences! In the same way, if we don't invest in God's word, we'll end up with something much more serious than painful blisters and aching knees: we'll end up with painful consequences and aching hearts. Zipping out the door unequipped leaves us empty and too exhausted for running our daily course. Neglecting time in God's word is an invitation for damage, disaster, and ruin. Dear friend, I urge you to make the most crucial investment for your faith journey: embrace the word of God as the fuel that fires your very soul! The power of his word prepares you for the path ahead—thoroughly equipping you for every good work.

READY? Are you consistently spending time in God's word? Are you meditating on the power of his word throughout your day? If this is an area you are lacking in, what needs to change for this to be a priority? If you're walking through a difficult season, embrace his word to give you strength, hope, and peace.

GET SET. Psalm 119:10–11, 105 "I seek you with all my heart; do not let me stray from your commands. I have hidden your word in my heart that I might not sin against you. Your word is a lamp for my feet; a light for my path"

GO! *Dear God, I thank you for the gift of your word ... that I can hold it in my physical hands and turn the pages with ease. Forgive me for the times I've ignored your word. Please ignite a passion in my heart to embrace it like never before. Help me remember the power that comes from it. May your word be firmly planted and deeply rooted in every area of my life. Amen.*

A TIME TO RUN AND A TIME TO WALK

Isaiah 40:31 "Those who hope in the Lord will renew their strength. They will soar on wings like eagles; they will run and not grow weary, they will walk and not be faint."

Many runners can run continuously from start to finish without ever slowing down. But that strategy doesn't fit everyone. When training for my first half-marathon, I'd gotten up to four miles without stopping. My heart soared with pride, but my knees seared with pain! After getting advice from seasoned runners, I attempted a strategy from expert Jeff Galloway[1]. His premise is that if you incorporate short walks in between spurts of running, you'll avoid exhaustion and injury. It also conserves your body's resources and allows for quicker recovery.

Now I run for five minutes and walk for one minute. After falling into this routine, I realized two crucial things.

First, this strategy gave my knees a rest in between my spurts of running. I was able to increase my mileage each week without any further discomfort. No pain!

Second, I realized these short breaks of walking gave me a *mental* break. Instead of thinking, *Wow—I've got to run multiple miles today*, it was easier to think, *Okay—I can run for the next five minutes, but then I'll get a break.* I embraced this strategy! Much more doable than running full force without stopping.

Who are we to think we can keep running and not slow down on this journey of faith we find ourselves on? We falsely think we can keep going at a breakneck pace, but God designed us to intentionally slow down at specific times on our race of faith. One minute walks paint a picture of our time to be still with God. Life is often weary. We feel as if we'll faint at the next announcement of bad news. We are so easily overcome with stress, worry, and anxiety. But when we continue at full steam with no intention of slowing down, we feel overcome with exhaustion and pain we simply can't handle.

We must be intentional in carving out time with Jesus. Time to rest. Time to be renewed and refreshed. Time to just be still in his presence. We're called to soar like an eagle, not rage mindlessly like a hamster on a wheel. Our quiet time with him prepares us to go back out on the course of life and keep going. Our time in prayer keeps us connected with him, allowing us to breathe easier when life unexpectedly shakes us up.

This whole run–walk approach gives us a new perspective on how we ought to view the challenges that seem insurmountable at different seasons of life. When it says in Isaiah 40:31 that we soar on wings like an eagle, it means we get an eagle's perspective. Just as an eagle soars *above* the storm and sees the bigger picture, we too can get that same perspective if our hope is truly in God. So when I get overwhelmed with a long-term challenge facing me, I can choose to run and not grow weary. I can choose to walk and not faint. Why? Because my hope is in him.

READY? Is there an area of your life where God is asking you to slow down? Where do you need to walk with God instead of running in your own strength? Take time to be still before him so he can give you the eagle's perspective.

GET SET. Proverbs 4:12 "When you walk, your steps will not be hampered; when you run, you will not stumble."

GO! *Lord Jesus, please help me to slow down and be still before you. Forgive me for the times I haven't paused in your presence and sought your help. I humbly ask you to renew my strength. When I'm weary and faint, help me to thank you for the hope you've promised me. Amen.*

AT THE CRACK OF DAWN

Psalm 5:3 "In the morning, Lord, you hear my voice; in the morning I lay my requests before you and wait expectantly."

Darkness hovers. Most people still slumber in deep sleep. Our alarm clock blares. Eyes widening, we quickly bound out of bed. Careful not to wake anyone else in the house, we throw on our clothes. We're ready to do what we planned all along. It's the crack of dawn. Time to run.

Why is it that we runners choose to run so darn early? For heaven's sake, it's still dark outside! Our nonrunner family members and friends question our motives to exchange another hour of sleep to run. Why not run later in the day when it's not so, umm, *dark*?

Most runners claim that it's beneficial to run in the early morning hours before other things start to interfere. Once the demands of the work day are underway or kids are bounding out of bed, it can be much harder to squeeze in a run. Feeling wiped out after a demanding day, the thought of running later in the day can seem daunting.

Running in the early morning gets your metabolism geared up for the rest of the day. Energy you didn't have at first rushes through your blood vessels and you're suddenly ready to face the day ahead with a more positive attitude. You're also more likely to be aware of the food you put into your mouth after putting in hard work.

Runners claim it's worth getting up early to see a sunrise first thing in the morning. The beauty and sheer joy of watching the sun come up is invigorating. Breathing in the cool air of the morning. Breathing out gratitude for such an awesome part of creation. With a refreshed perspective, you're more able to tackle the day ahead.

While running early in the morning is good, seeking God in our first waking moments is even better. David writes that his requests are brought to the Lord *in the morning* (Psalm 5:3). Early in the morning before we fall into our breakneck pace of life, we are urged to put our focus on God. *Before* we get distracted with work and interruptions from our kids. *Before* we start tackling our to-do list. *Before* we pick up our phone to check social media.

Seeking God first puts everything in perspective. Fixing our eyes on him before anything or anyone else grabs our attention sets the pace for the rest of the day. Humbly acknowledging him first allows the Holy Spirit to flow more freely through every part of your soul. Asking for his guidance makes us more cautious about what we choose to put into our mind throughout the day.

Even Jesus got up early in the morning to spend time with his heavenly Father. He was fully man and fully God, yet he modeled for us what we should embrace *first* upon waking. His example should challenge us to follow in his footsteps. Footsteps that ran to God early in the morning.

It's well worth rising early to encounter Jesus. Sitting still in his presence washes peace and joy over us like nothing else can. The power he infuses upon us is invigorating. We can then breathe in his grace. And this prepares us to breathe out praise to him throughout the rest of the day. Before we start our day, we're refreshed with an eternal perspective. He prepares us to not just tackle the day ahead, but to thrive in it!

READY? How are you doing with spending time with God before your day gets going? Are there any changes you need to make in your schedule? How does spending quality time with God affect the rest of your day?

GET SET. Mark 1:35 "Very early in the morning, while it was still dark, Jesus got up, left the house, and went off to a solitary place, where he prayed."

GO! *Lord Jesus, thank you for the truth of your word. Help me to realize the importance of acknowledging you first in the morning. Forgive me for the times I've put other things ahead of you. Help me carve out the time to be still in your presence. Praise you for the promise that when we seek you first, you will provide all that we need. Amen.*

TIME TO SPRINT!

1 Peter 5:8 "Be alert and of sober mind. Your enemy the devil prowls around like a roaring lion looking for someone to devour."

Breathing in the fresh, cool air, I basked in the warmth of the sun. Just a couple more miles and I'd head back home. Soaking up the moment, I slowed my pace to take it all in.

Suddenly, out of nowhere, I heard an ear-piercing noise stopping me in my tracks. Turning around quickly, I spotted a brown blitz of fur in the distance. Surely this tiny creature posed no harm. But the dog rushed toward me, barking louder, teeth snarled. A surge of energy rose up within me. Like a caged bull suddenly released, I pounded the pavement, sprinting like crazy to escape this pesky dog! Heart thumping out of my chest, I didn't even look back. I kept running until I no longer heard the ear-piercing bark. After running another half-mile, I slowed down, catching my breath. Although it would lengthen my run, I took a different route home.

If you've never faced the threat of a loose dog, your chances are pretty good if you're planning on making running a habit. Besides loose dogs on the run, what else drives us to abandon our rhythmic pace and flee? An unexpected thunderstorm? A stalker? Perhaps something else has demanded your sudden need to sprint. Whatever it is, in these situations we've got to *flee*!

When running our race of life, what does God's word command us to flee from? We are called to flee the evil desires of youth (2 Timothy 2:22), the love of money (1 Timothy 6:10–11), idolatry (1 Corinthians 10:14), and sexual immorality (1 Corinthians 6:18).

Our response to these potential sins is to *flee*. The word "flee" has the following meanings: "to take flight, retreat, escape, bolt, seek safety through flight, or run away from." When evil stares us in the face, it doesn't mean we stand around and check it out, watching to see what will happen. No, dear friend, we should kick it in high gear and run away from these things with all our might.

Although the world embraces these things, God urges us to run in the opposite direction. Sin often appears innocent from far away. *Surely this won't harm me!* But if we stand still, allowing it to approach us, we suddenly realize the power it has. And before we know it, we're caught in the grip of sin's clenched teeth.

You'll hear different strategies on rushing dogs, but in regards to *prevention*, veteran runners agree on this: know your route and avoid streets where you know loose dogs could pose a threat. Just as runners take precautions in avoiding potentially dangerous situations, we can apply the same strategy in the area of *temptation*. Remember that temptation is not a sin. But our response to it can lead to sin if we're not careful.

In 1 Peter 5:8, we're warned about our enemy. Satan prowls around like a lion waiting to devour us. He looks for an opportune time—a weak moment—to attack. He's just like that pesky dog waiting to pounce on distracted runners. When we know our weaknesses, we can avoid situations that set us up for temptation. We can pray and proceed with caution. Pursuing the path of righteousness might take us the long way around, but it's better than traipsing down the path of sin.

Avoiding all temptation is *ideal*, but you'd better be ready for those sudden moments—when your feet must sprint!

READY? Identify a recent time when temptation caught you off guard. What was your response? Is there a current situation in your life causing you to feel tempted? What next step can you take to stay on a safer path? Is it harder for you to avoid temptation or escape sin in the moment?

GET SET. 1 Corinthians 10:14 "Therefore, my dear friends, flee from idolatry." (Also read 1 Timothy 6:10–11, 2 Timothy 2:22, and 1 Corinthians 6:18)

GO! *Thank you Jesus that you understand temptation. In those moments when I am tempted, equip me with strength and power from your word. Help me stay alert when the enemy seeks to attack. Praise you for your promise of victory. Amen.*

WHAT'S YOUR PACE?

Hebrews 12:1 "Let us run with endurance the race that is set before us, looking unto Jesus, the author and finisher of our faith...."

"What's your pace?" This is a common question you'll frequently hear among fellow runners. It's also a question most registration forms require you to answer when signing up for a race. So what's the big deal about your pace? Why do we place so much emphasis on knowing exactly how many minutes it takes us to cover a mile? The reality is that we all run (and walk) at different paces. Some are out to win the race—dashing off like a bolt of lightning. Some have accepted the fact that they will be bringing up the rear—the back of the pack. Perhaps you fall somewhere in between these two extremes.

Could I run at a faster pace at the start of a long race? Absolutely! Could I maintain that pace throughout the *entire race*? Absolutely NOT! If I started off sprinting with all my might, I'd wear out quickly, draining all my energy before I'd reach the finish line. So I pace myself, refusing to focus on those passing me quickly. My pace will probably fluctuate throughout the race, but that's okay. My determination is focused on finishing the race—at my own unique pace.

Each runner is built differently with a unique speed, stride, and stamina. Similarly, we are each designed by God with different talents, attributes, and personalities. He didn't create you to run someone else's race. He created you to run *your* race, at your own *unique pace.* If I strive to measure up with someone who's further ahead in her journey of life, I'll crash and burn with exhaustion. Imagine a couch-to-5K runner attempting to run alongside an elite marathoner. Crazy, right? But that's a picture of what we do when we strive to run someone else's pace in life.

The pressure to run someone else's pace often comes from within. But sometimes it comes from others. Imagine a group of seasoned marathoners running a seven-minute mile. They look back at a runner who's averaging a ten-minute mile and yell, "Hurry up, slow-poke! Get up here and run with us!" Sound absurd? Now transfer that scenario to real life. Have we ever allowed others to place unrealistic expectations upon us? We cave in and begin running a pace we weren't meant to run. Sure we might bolt out confidently at first, but as time goes on, our physical and emotional energy fizzles out—draining our motivation and sense of purpose.

Whatever is driving us to run someone else's pace, it's not good if it isn't where God wants us. We were designed to live this life at the unique pace God calls us to. Don't waste your energy catching up with someone else. Don't get caught up in the sprinting crowd when it's time for you to slow down. Resolve to thrive in the race of life. One step at a time. In your unique pace!

READY? Are you content with the pace you're running in your physical race? How about in your faith journey? Are there any areas of your life where you feel you might be trying to run someone else's pace? Can you identify anyone who's pressuring you to run *their pace*? Spend some time in prayer asking God to help you discover your pace.

GET SET. Galatians 5:25 "Since we live by the spirit, let us keep in step with the spirit."

GO! *Dear God, I confess that sometimes I try to run my race of faith at a pace you simply did not design me for. Forgive me for running in my own power instead of relying on the Holy Spirit. Help me surrender completely to the purpose you created me for as I run with endurance each step of the way. Amen.*

THROUGH THE STORM

Isaiah 43:2 "When you pass through the waters, I will be with you; and when you pass through the rivers, they will not sweep over you. When you walk through the fire, you will not be burned; the flames will not set you ablaze."

I absolutely love running under a clear-blue sky, sun beaming overhead. Cold weather? No problem. But I utterly *despise* running in the rain. If it's raining the least little bit during training, I happily opt for my elliptical machine or head to an indoor track.

One spring I'd trained for the Country Music half-marathon in Nashville. The day before the race, the weather forecast did not look favorable. The 95 percent chance of rain left a slim possibility for clear skies. I prayed like crazy for those gloomy clouds to quickly disappear. In one final, desperate plea, I prayed for the rain to at least hold off until I finished my race.

Come on, God, really? Can't you make it stop raining for just a few hours? Don't you know I hate running in the rain?

As the start time approached, the weather forecast remained the same and I had to finally accept the sad reality ... I was going to get *wet*. Anxiously pulling a rain poncho over my body, I hoped this flimsy piece of plastic would keep me dry from the raging downpour. Boy, was I wrong! Huddling up together with a sea of 30,000 runners, I anxiously awaited my turn to arrive at the start line. The steady rain drenching my socks and shoes, I inched my way forward. After a grueling thirty-minute wait, I was finally off and running. The driving rain felt like torrential flood as I sloshed through puddles the *entire* thirteen miles of that race.

Halfway through the race, I flung off the heavy rain poncho. My attempt to stay dry proved futile. The sound of rain drumming the pavement almost drowned out the music I was listening to on my iPod, but I could still hear the gentle whisper of my Heavenly Father above the noise.

Lisa, just as I am with you in this pouring rain, I am with you through all the storms of your life. Sometimes I calm the storm around you, but sometimes I allow you to go through it. Although you'll get wet, I promise to be with you.

Drenched and shivering on the outside, I finished the race. But an inward peace had saturated my soul, ushered in by God's truth. Once you've run through a constant downpour, the scattered showers don't seem to bother you as much as they did before. And the same is true in our walk of faith. Once we've waddled through a heart-wrenching storm, we come out stronger on the other side. Our faith grows. Our perspective changes. Today's key verse doesn't say *if* you pass through the waters; it clearly says *when* (Isaiah 43:2). When the violent storms of life gush over us, we can trust that he will be with us *through* it all.

So what about you? What storm are you sloshing through? Are you begging God to remove your difficult circumstances? Are you trying to keep from "getting wet" with your own human devices? Or can you humbly accept that he might take you *through* the storm? Maybe you're drenched at the start line and the storm is raging. Maybe you're in the middle and you feel like you'll drown in worry and fear. No matter where you are or whatever the storm is, he promises to carry us *through* it.

READY? Can you identify some past storms God has brought you through? How can you apply the wisdom you gained from these past storms to a current storm you are in now? If you are resisting a storm, are you ready to embrace it with absolute trust in God?

GET SET. Matthew 5:45 "He causes his sun to rise on the evil and the good, and sends rain on the righteous and the unrighteous."

GO! *Heavenly Father, I confess my selfish desire for you to remove all the storms in my life. Help me trust you when your plan is not to calm the storm, but to calm my anxious heart in the midst of the storm. Thank you for promising to walk with me through all the storms in my life. Amen.*

WATER STOPS

Psalm 42:1 "As the deer pants for streams of water, so my soul thirsts for you, my God."

Mile marker one. Mile marker three. Mile marker five. These are etched in your mind. Why? These are the official water stops for your upcoming race. You know *exactly* where they are. For most races, you can locate these specific spots online. They're crucial. You wouldn't survive without them. They aren't just randomly placed without thought along the course. They are intentional. Purposeful. Strategically positioned exactly where they need to be. On race day, you breathe a sigh of relief as the first water stop comes into your view. Race volunteers line the road, holding out plastic cups of water. Grabbing a cup, you gulp down every last drop. Your thirst is immediately quenched. Feeling refreshed, you continue on with confidence, knowing there's another water stop up ahead in a few more miles.

Dehydration would easily set in without your water stops. No matter how fast-paced you are, without water stops you would crash and burn. You usually know about how far you can run before your body needs water. Continue past that point and you start to wear down. Even when you're training, you plan out *when* and *where* you'll get water. Running around the block, you place a bottle of water by your mailbox as you circle around a familiar path. Running with friends, perhaps you run a specific circuit and return to your cars for a fill-up. Sometimes organized groups set up tables for runners at specific points. Whatever the case may be, you strategically plan for water when you need to be refreshed.

Do we have the same urgency on our journey of faith? Do we intentionally plan *spiritual* water stops? Places of rest for quenching the thirst of our weary souls. Refreshment is vital for the long road ahead. We all need to plan accordingly! What exactly does a water stop look like on your faith journey? It could be attending a worship service on the weekend. Perhaps it's a weekly Bible study or an accountability group. Prayer time with a few close friends. Meeting a fellow believer for coffee or calling a trusted friend. Carving out time to get away from the chaos and stress. Each of these is purposeful—giving refreshment when we're weary. They are like a pit stop on the journey of faith.

Waiting until things fall apart before seeking out these places of rest would be like running aimlessly without any thought of where your water is going to come from! I've never met a runner who wasn't intentional with their water supply. Just as the water stops on a race course are strategically positioned, we too as Christ followers must be *intentional* when it comes to discipleship and staying strong in our faith. We get weary. Life sometimes feels like a drought. We must be purposeful in planning out where we will stop to be renewed, refreshed, and refueled!

READY? Can you identify specific water stops in your faith journey? Are you stopping often enough or do you need to add some more stops to your course? How does having water stops affect the level of peace and hope you have when things get tough? If you don't have any water stops, pray and ask God to show you who, where, and when they might be.

GET SET. Matthew 11:28–29 "Come to me, all you who are weary and burdened and I will give you rest. Take my yoke upon you and learn from me, for I am gentle and humble in heart, and you will find rest for your souls." (Also read Jeremiah 31:25)

GO! *Heavenly Father, I praise you for being my ultimate water stop on my path of life. Help me to humbly embrace the water stops you've put into my life. Help me reach out to others when I'm feeling weary. Thank you for refreshing my soul with the power of your word. Amen.*

WHO'S AHEAD OF YOU?

Galatians 6:2 "Carry each other's burdens, and in this way you will fulfill the law of Christ."

Just when you think you've arrived at your fastest pace, whoosh!—another runner speeds past you like a bolt of lightning. You can almost feel a breeze from the force of their speed. You see them quickly disappear from your view and, before you know it, they're long gone. *How in the world does she keep up that pace? I'll never be able to catch up!*

Unless you're the first one to cross the finish line in a race, there's always going to be someone running ahead of you. We are definitely called to run at our own pace, but that doesn't mean we can't learn from others who are ahead of us. Beginning runners seek out training tips from veteran runners. Runners who've sustained their first injuries could gain valuable wisdom from others who survived those same injuries. The first race ushers in a wave of anxious nerves. *What should I expect? What should I wear for this kind of weather?* Who else out there would know answers to these questions? Runners ahead of you! Their pace may not necessarily be faster than you, but they've pounded the pavement far longer than you have. Instead of putting them in an unreachable category, those of us who are behind them could instead reach out, asking for guidance and insight.

If you're a follower of Christ, there's always going to be someone ahead of you—further up the path of life. People who have been following Christ for many years longer. People who have long ago passed through the very same season you may be walking through now. People who have much wisdom and insight to offer if only we will ask. As you enter into a difficult season, perhaps a wave of anxiety is rushing into the depth of your weary soul. *How will I ever get through this? Will I ever make it to the other side?* And then you may wonder with great curiosity: WHO do I know that perhaps has ventured through this same kind of challenge?

Let me tell you without a doubt that someone is ahead of you who can gently and lovingly guide you. Maybe it's an older mom who survived the season of raising teenagers. Maybe it's the woman you've heard about who survived her nasty divorce and is on the other side now. Whatever challenge you may be facing, you're more likely to gain peace and strength with someone else helping you through. So go ahead. Reach out. Ask. Humbly wave the white flag of your soul and courageously say, "I need your help!"

In the Bible we meet a young man named Timothy, a new believer who needed some direction. The apostle Paul was running his race ahead of Timothy. Paul poured his very life into this young man (2 Timothy 3:10-11). Without Paul, Timothy would've floundered in his faith. Grown weary. Lost his hope. But instead he clung to Paul. He humbled himself and listened with a teachable heart. And then he flourished into a bold teacher of the gospel. He could keep running his race at a fierce pace because he walked in the footsteps of Paul (2 Timothy 2:2). Who's ahead of *you*?

READY? Identify an area of your life where you feel challenged and could use some guidance. Ask God to show you someone who has walked through a similar challenge. Are you willing to reach out and ask for help? Pray and ask God for strength and wisdom to take the next step.

GET SET. Proverbs 1:5 "A wise man will hear and increase in learning, and a man of understanding will acquire wise counsel." (Also read Proverbs 11:14)

GO! *Heavenly Father, this life can feel so difficult at times! I feel weary trying to navigate through the hard times on my own. You've called us to carry each other's burdens, so I humbly ask you to show me someone who's ahead of me, someone who can walk alongside me during this season of my life. Help me set aside any pride that may stand in the way. Amen.*

HURLING OFF THE HINDRANCES

Hebrews 12:1 "Let us throw off everything that hinders and the sin that so easily entangles...."

It's race day! A cold breeze gushes through the crowd. Runners quickly jog in place, struggling to stay warm. You can see your breath in the coolness of the air. Shivering, you count down the minutes until start time. Your outer layer will be discarded later, but for now it keeps you warm *before* the race.

The race finally begins and you're content with this outer layer. It fits snugly around you, giving immediate warmth and comfort. But then something happens. Your body thaws out, gradually heating up to a full sweat. This shirt you earlier couldn't do without now feels cumbersome, causing much distress. You're ready to throw it off. You literally peel it off and toss it, knowing you'll never see it again. But at this point you don't care because you can run with more ease and freedom. Getting rid of the sweat shirt lightens your load.

As you continue running along the race course, you notice a mass of shirts and jackets strewn across both edges of the road. You realize you're among other runners who know this truth: you can't run efficiently unless you throw off the things that weigh you down.

Should we not have this same attitude with our sins? The hindrances entangling us, weighing us down—they utterly leave us burdened and miserable, but we often convince ourselves we're okay with them. We think they'll keep us comfortable, snug, and protected from the cold, distant world. But we can only go so far before we start to realize we're getting uncomfortable. Our soul is miserable with this added weight. We feel burdened with anguish. Feelings of defeat hinder us from walking in victory.

Today's verse tells us to literally *throw off* our sins (Hebrews 12:1). A runner who's fallen into her perfect stride isn't going to slow down, prance over to the side of the road, and neatly lay her old sweat shirt down. Of course not! Just when she notices the change in her body temperature and feels the heat inside, she knows it's time. She quickly peels off the cumbersome sweat shirt, tugging furiously to get it over her head and, with all her might, fling it as far away from her as possible.

This picture is what we are called to do with sin. Just when we recognize the change in our thoughts, the change in our heart, the change in our attitude—we detect something isn't right. Misery engulfs us. Maybe it's selfish thoughts. Perhaps it's a prideful action hurting our loved ones. Or maybe we lash out with angry words, defending our way of doing things. Then we feel weighed down with guilt we weren't meant to carry. Anguish rises up inside. When we recognize this, that's when we grab the ugly thing it really is and strip it off.

We hurl it out of sight and into the forgiving arms of Jesus. He's strong enough to catch those sins we've thrown at him along our path. He has the power to forgive and redeem because of what he did on the cross. And then he does something incredible: he hurls our forgiven sins completely away from us ... never to be seen again.

READY? What are you allowing to hinder your walk with Jesus? Are you clinging tightly to a certain sin? Are you ready to call it what it is and throw it off? Ask God to show you what is weighing you down so you can cast it off and run your race in victory.

GET SET. Psalm 103:12 "As far as the east is from the west, he has removed our sins from us."

GO! *Lord Jesus, show me the sins I'm allowing to weigh me down. Help me acknowledge them before you. I confess them now and ask your forgiveness. Soften my heart so I can be more sensitive to the sins that grieve your heart. Help me let go of anything that keeps me from walking in victory. Amen.*

TAKING A WRONG TURN

Psalm 25:4–5 "Show me your ways, Oh Lord; teach me your paths. Guide me in your truth and teach me for you are God my savior and my hope is in you all day long."

While vacationing on a beautiful beach in Florida, I'd planned on running three miles. The first two were under nicely shaded shops along the boardwalk, but then I wanted to enjoy the scenery of ocean waves crashing upon the beach. *I'll run my last mile along the shore and call it quits.* Sounded like a good plan to me. I trudged over across the sand to the edge of the shore where I could run on solid ground. My plan was to run for half a mile out and half a mile back to make it an even three. But that's when I got off course.

I was ready to head back the last half mile and cut back through where I *thought* I'd entered the beach area. But what I didn't know *then* was that I'd turned too soon. As I jogged back to where I thought our condo was located, the scenery around me didn't look familiar. I kept looking for the sign that bore the name of our condo, but I didn't see it anywhere. My persistent jog slowly turned to a sluggish stroll. I finally had to humbly admit the truth: I had taken a wrong turn and was headed in the *opposite* direction.

The sweltering sun ushered streams of sweat running down my back—joined with tears of frustration pouring down my face. No longer underneath shaded shops, I couldn't escape the blistering sun.

I sensed God gently speaking to my weary soul: *Yes, you are turned around. But that doesn't define who you are.*

As I continued to walk one step at a time closer to my condo, I asked God to show me some truth from this situation so it wouldn't be a total waste. (Of course, the obvious lesson is to figure out where you are *before* running an extra mile!)

Sometimes we think we know *exactly* where we are in life. We head off in a certain direction without evaluating where we really are. We make plans and think we have it all figured out, but then we suddenly realize we're not where we intended to be. We have to admit we took a wrong turn. We have to set our pride aside and accept the reality that we missed something.

The cool thing about God is that even when we've taken a wrong turn, he's still right there with us. Even when we're way off his intended course for us, he sees where we are. We may have to take a longer route to get back on track, but he promises to never leave us.

Although I was running in unfamiliar territory, I still felt the effects of the sun. In fact, it was the only thing recognizable in my moment of bewilderment. Whether I'm running on my home turf in Kentucky or on a sandy beach in Florida, the same sun shines down on me. And in the same way, God is always with us whether we're in a predictable routine or right smack in the middle of something frightening and unfamiliar.

READY? Recall a time you were running in unfamiliar territory. What was the outcome? Identify a time in your life when you ended up at a point you didn't intend. How did you respond? If you've recently taken a wrong turn, are you willing to let God reroute your path?

GET SET. 1 John 1:9 "If we confess our sins, he is faithful and just and will cleanse us from all unrighteousness."

GO! *Heavenly Father, show me in my life where I've gotten off course. Reveal to me anything I need to confess. Thank you for your faithfulness to me even when I'm going the wrong direction. Help me run back into your loving arms and walk confidently in your forgiveness and love. Amen.*

READY FOR THE BATTLE

Ephesians 6:11–12 "Put on the full armor of God so that you will be able to stand firm against the schemes of the devil. For our struggle is not against flesh and blood, but against the rulers, against the powers, against the world forces of this darkness, against the spiritual forces of wickedness in the heavenly places."

The night before a race, adrenaline pumps through your body, anticipation building. In preparation for running out the door at the crack of dawn, you strategically organize your gear just right. From head to toe, every single item is laid out in clear view to make sure nothing is overlooked: hat, shirt, shorts, socks, shoes, Body Glide, iPod, and your GPS watch. If any of these items is forgotten, you'll struggle to run your race. Each item has a distinct purpose—designed for a specific job to protect you. When your alarm blares loudly in the morning, you're ready to grab your essentials and confidently head out the door. You can't fathom not being prepared! You fully understand what's at stake.

A hat protects you from the blistering sun. Your wicking shirt and shorts soak up moisture—keeping your skin dry. You'd never dream of wearing cotton! Your pricey running socks and Body

Glide are worth every penny, protecting your feet from blisters. Your running shoes give you ample support for pounding the pavement. You've downloaded the perfect songs on your playlist, trusting they'll motivate you throughout the race. Your GPS watch is fully charged, ready to keep you on track. A wise runner is fully prepared—ready to conquer the race ahead, like a soldier armed for battle.

But there's another battle that should get our full attention. We're told in Ephesians 6:11—18 about a *spiritual* battle. This battle threatens *every believer* in Christ. It's ugly. It's fierce. And we'd be foolish to ignore it. When it comes to preparing for this battle, are we putting as much emphasis on the armor of God as we are with our running gear? Do we intentionally ponder the powerful pieces of armor God has designed for us? Are we carelessly rushing into challenges and difficulties without any thought of our protection? If so, we are setting ourselves up for disaster. And in this case the disaster is much more serious than sunburn and blisters!

Each piece of armor is designed with precision to arm us for battle. Our *helmet of salvation* symbolizes what Christ did for us on the cross (Ephesians 6:17). In Biblical times it stood for a sign of military strength. The *breastplate of righteousness* allows us to walk confidently—not in our own power, but in the righteousness of Jesus (Ephesians 6:14). What about the *girdle of truth*? Without this, we don't stand a chance against the deception of the world and the ploys of the enemy (Ephesians 6:14). We must cling to the truth of who we are in Christ. The *shoes of peace* allow us to demonstrate love to a hurting world (Ephesians 6:15). *The shield of faith* is the most important defensive weapon we have. It protects us in the heat of battle, extinguishing all the flaming arrows hurled our way from the enemy (Ephesians 6:16). And last but not least, we must firmly grip the *sword of the spirit*— the only offensive weapon given to us (Ephesians 6:17). With it we demolish the temptations set out to distract and destroy us.

So the next time you're laying out your physical running gear, let it remind you and inspire you to be prepared for the spiritual battle within your soul. Ready or not, the battle awaits you.

READY? Are you being intentional in putting on your spiritual armor? Reflect on each piece of armor and how it can empower you for life's challenges. What steps do you need to take to ensure you're completely dressed for battle?

GET SET. 1 Peter 5:8 "Be self-controlled and alert. Your enemy the devil prowls around like a roaring lion looking for someone to devour." (Also read Ephesians 6:13–18)

GO! *Dear Jesus, thank you for giving me each piece of armor. I desperately come before you and ask you to remind me of the power you've given me through each of these. Help me humble myself as I put on each piece and walk victoriously each day of my life on this earth. Amen.*

IN ALL CONDITIONS

Philippians 4:11–13 "I have learned to be content whatever the circumstances. I know what it is to be in need, and I know what it is to have plenty. I have learned the secret of being content in any and every situation, whether well fed or hungry, whether living in plenty or in want. I can do all this through him who gives me strength."

What are the perfect conditions when pounding the pavement? Ideal weather. No aches and pains. Fastest pace ever. When we're fortunate enough to run in ultimate conditions, we soak it up—savoring every moment. This is what we call the runner's high. This is when we tell anyone who'll listen, "Running is the best thing ever!" Our best-case-scenario runs make us feel on top of the world, like nothing could ever steal our passion.

But what if it's below freezing? Frigid wind blowing in your face. How about rain? Not just scattered showers, but a torrential downpour—sloshing through puddles, water streaming down your face. Does your passion begin to melt when running in blistering heat? Maybe you run your slowest pace ever in a race, knees throbbing at the finish line. How do you survive your worst-case-scenario kind of runs?

We can't control extreme weather. But we adjust our wardrobe—acclimating to the outside temps. The temps remain the same, but our attitude changes our perception. Our bodies won't always function the way we want. But we recover and keep going.

As Christians, we can apply these same strategies in our difficult seasons of life. We can't control the circumstances swirling around us, but we can choose to be content in every situation. Is that really possible? According to the apostle Paul, it is.

His journey led him down a path of extreme persecution. He was flogged, beaten with rods, stoned, and thrown into prison multiple times. He plunged through other worst-case-scenario seasons, too! He was shipwrecked three times, spent an entire night and day in the open sea, faced danger from robbers and frequently experienced thirst, hunger, and sleepless nights (2 Corinthians 11:23—28). (Imagine showing up to a race start line completely dehydrated, famished, and exhausted!)

He couldn't control the extreme persecution he faced, yet he chose to be content—even in prison, where he penned many pages of the New Testament epistles. Even in horrendous circumstances, he accepted where he was. How in the world could he possibly do that?

The key is found in today's scripture: he could do all things *through Christ* (Philippians 4:13). The power of the Holy Spirit ignited a supernatural strength within him, allowing his soul to acclimate to his surroundings.

Although we long for perfect living conditions, that's not reality. We don't always get to live life in our sweet spot. Just as our physical bodies acclimate to extreme temps, Jesus pours his strength and peace on our weary souls. When we embrace the Holy Spirit, he leads us in every situation, no matter how extreme it feels. As strength ignites within us, it changes our perception of what lies ahead.

We must embrace Paul's words and trust that we *can* do all things through Christ. When life's bitter-cold winds blow fiercely in our face, we keep moving. When the journey feels like a desert, we seek the streams of living water. When hard times slow us down, we don't give up. We keep on trusting and staying as close to Jesus as possible. No matter what kind of season we're facing, we resolve to keep running the race.

READY? Identify a time when life's conditions were not so good for you. How did you get through it? Where in your life are you struggling to be content right now? Like Paul, are you willing to surrender, claiming the strength of Jesus?

GET SET. 2 Corinthians 12:10 "For the sake of Christ, then I am content with weaknesses, insults, hardships, persecutions and calamities. For when I am weak, then I am strong."

GO! *Lord Jesus, I thank you for the reminder today of your powerful strength. When I feel like drowning in difficult circumstances, help me cling to your truth. Instead of focusing on the stuff I can't control, please help me focus on who you are. Amen.*

THE DAY OF REST

Exodus 20:8–10 "Remember to observe the Sabbath day by keeping it holy. You have six days each week for your ordinary work, but the seventh day is a Sabbath day of rest dedicated to the Lord your God."

Most runners follow a strict training schedule when a race is on the horizon. Short runs. Strength training. Cross training. And of course the weekly long runs. All these pieces of the runner's puzzle work together, each one fulfilling a specific role to ensure success. But something crucial that simply can't be overlooked is the day of *rest*. Most training schedules have this word in bold letters, calling attention to its importance.

At first I didn't understand why this day of rest was part of the runner's world. Shouldn't I be *doing* something? What if I got behind earlier in the week and needed to squeeze in a quick three-mile run or weightlifting session? Couldn't I use that day to get *ahead* in my training? What could it possibly hurt? Besides, I didn't even feel tired.

It is no surprise that the day of rest usually comes the day after a long run. Your physical body needs this day to recuperate from the stress placed upon it. It's a crucial day to recover. A day to let your legs relax, unwinding from the persistent impact of constant pounding. A runner's body requires time for repair. Miss this day and you're setting yourself up for injury. Ignore the warning and you'll surely regret it later.

Just as our physical bodies require rest to recover, our souls desperately crave a day of rest as well. After living a full week at a breakneck pace, we really need to slow down. God beckons us to step off the crazy treadmill and just be still in his presence. We must pull away from our hectic schedule, unplug from the rest of the world, and bask in his loving presence. We might be bombarded with a nagging urge to use this day of rest for getting caught up on errands—to get ahead. But we simply can't do so! We've got to embrace the truth that our God designed us to *rest*. He set the example for us when he created the world. On the seventh day, he ceased from his work. He rested. If God set the pace for us in this area, then shouldn't we embrace it and obediently follow after him?

But I have so much to do! I need to get caught up on work, errands and projects! I feel so guilty resting when everything is piling up around me!

He calls us to unplug from our crazy pace. He invites us to simply sit at his feet. We inwardly shout, *I'm trying to survive!* but he whispers, "I want you to *thrive*." He desires to recharge, renew, and refresh us—but he can't if we ignore our day of rest. We bypass many blessings when we ignore the call to rest. Like a runner's body suffers harm without rest, our souls ache deeply and our faith is weakened. Don't settle for what you think is *good*. Surrender to God's best—a day of *rest*!

READY? Are you carving out a day of rest from your busy schedule? Is it easier for you to justify physical rest compared to soul rest? Why or why not? What changes do you need to make for making time to rest? The next time you notice the word REST on your training schedule, let it remind you to embrace God's day of rest.

GET SET. Matthew 11:28 "Come to me all who are weary and burdened and I will give you rest."

GO! *Lord Jesus, I struggle sometimes with embracing a day of rest in the quick-paced culture we live in. Help me to slow down and pull away from the cares of this world. Please help me embrace this day to worship you and be renewed by your peace. Thank you for designing my life with a built-in desire to rest in your presence. Amen.*

TRUDGING UP THE STEEP HILLS

Psalm 121:1 "I lift up my eyes to the hills, where does my help come from? My help comes from the Lord, maker of heaven and earth."

Hal Higdon, running writer and coach, says this about running hills: "Hills. We love them. We hate them. They make us strong. They make us weak. Today I choose to embrace hills."[2] It's painful when you're trudging up a steep hill! Every fiber of your leg muscles tighten. You feel as if you won't make it to the top. Your calf muscles silently scream, *Please stop! We can't go another step!*

There's something invigorating about reaching the top of a steep hill. I finally look up from the ground and realize I've made it! Trudging up that hill caused my heart to almost pound out of my chest. My rapid breathing finally slows down. I let out a sigh of relief. Yes! The ground ahead of me begins to level out now. It's smooth and I can catch a glimpse of what's up ahead.

But I take a moment and turn around. *Did I really just come all this way?* I stand in awe of the beauty around me. Depending on the season, I might be looking at lush-green trees lining the path behind me, blue sky overhead. At other times I might be looking at autumn leaves splattered with bright orange-red colors. My absolute favorite view at the top of the hill is in winter, the snow-covered trees glistening in the sparkling light of the sun. These breathtaking views couldn't be seen from the bottom. I breathe in the fresh air, truly enjoying the moment.

I like how Eamonn Coughlin, three-time Irish Olympian, puts it: "Running hills breaks up your rhythm and forces your muscles to adapt to different stresses. The result? You become a stronger runner."[3]

The journey of life is also scattered with hills. Some of them I'd rather forget about. But I can undoubtedly say that there's something invigorating about finally making it to the top. Those trials I thought for sure would kill my soul and squash my spirit. Yes, there are times my heart has nearly broken, fiercely pounding out of my chest. My flesh shouting, *I can't go another step!* But when I reached the height of the trial, my anxious breathing slowed down. My tears and anguish turned into joyous breaths of praise. Praise to my Lord Jesus who walked beside me each step of the way.

Did I really just come all this way? I stood in awe of the beauty. Not physical surroundings, but the beauty of what God had done *in me*. The beauty of the strength he equipped me with. The beauty of his promise to never leave me or forsake me. My faith was strengthened. My hope was renewed. My love for him was magnified. And this view was something I wouldn't trade for anything. A view that couldn't be experienced without trudging up the steep hill.

READY? How does your physical body respond to hills? Are you trudging up a steep hill in your life right now? Does your heart ache and you just want to quit? I encourage you to tightly grip the loving arms of Jesus. Take a moment and think about the view awaiting you.

GET SET. Deuteronomy 31:6 "Be strong and courageous. Do not fear, for it is the Lord your God who goes with you. He will not leave you or forsake you."

GO! *Lord Jesus, the hills of this life are hard. Sometimes I just want to give up. When I feel this way, please help me remember your truth. Help me cling to the fact that you are with me even though I can't always see what's up at the top. Thank you for your promise of being with me each step of the way. Amen.*

WHAT'S ON YOUR PLAYLIST?

Romans 12:2 "Do not conform any longer to the pattern of this world, but be transformed by the renewing of your mind."

If you *must* run to music, then you consider your iPod or MP3player essential. Specific songs are selected with the intent of motivating—pumping you up when you need it most. Just when you recognize that familiar slump surging within you, one of your favorite tunes blasts away. Suddenly your mood is lifted and you feel new energy rising through every weary muscle of your body. The driving beat ignites your determination to keep going. Before you know it, you're running to the rhythm of the music and you have no intention of slowing down. Song after song keeps you going until you've reached your goal.

These songs on your playlist are carefully chosen. Not just any song will do! Can you imagine choosing songs with negative lyrics? Words that would insult you? Words of discouragement? Would you choose lullabies? Blues or slow-dance songs? Of course not! You'll choose songs with a driving beat. Songs with powerful words. Songs designed especially with running in mind.

According to some research in the runner's world, running to music can enhance your performance by making it feel easier, almost as if you could run faster and farther.[4] The songs you choose have the power to enhance your mood, invigorating you like nothing else could. Dr.Costas Karageorghis and Professor Peter Terry write in their book, *Inside Sport Psychology*, that listening to music while running can boost performance by up to 15 percent"[5]

What we listen to plays a huge part in how we run our race.

And so it is in our race of *faith*. What we choose to fix our mind on determines our thoughts. Our thoughts determine our attitudes. Our attitudes shape our behavior. And ultimately our behavior molds our character.

There are multiple voices clamoring for our attention daily: television, Internet, radio, and especially other people. We also hear whispers within our own ugly flesh and from the enemy. The voices we embrace are like the songs we choose to include on our playlists. When life gets tough and our weary soul can't go another step, what messages are going to blast into our mind? We have a choice as to which ones we'll tune into. If we listen to the negative talk of the world, we'll surely wear down and lose our momentum. But if we purposely choose God's gentle— yet powerful—voice, his truth will ignite our determination to persevere in his strength. It's critical that we tuck away truth into our mind so we don't fall for the lies of this world. When we feel a slump coming on, whatever is downloaded on our mental playlist determines whether we'll slow down or keep going.

Consider carefully what you download onto the playlist of your mind. Ultimately what goes into your mind will affect your soul. And the condition of your soul determines how you will spend the life God has graciously given you.

READY? Take a moment to reflect on the playlist of your mind. Which voices are the loudest? Are there any voices you need to delete? Ask God to guide you as you evaluate what you've been listening to.

GET SET. Philippians 4:8 "Finally, brothers, whatever is true, whatever is noble, whatever is right, whatever is pure, whatever is lovely, whatever is admirable—if anything is excellent or praiseworthy, think about such things" (Also read Colossians 3:2)

GO! *Heavenly Father, help me choose truth in the midst of this world's negativity. It's often hard to decipher through multiple voices calling out to me. Help me embrace your word and make it my filter. May your truth guide me all day long and lift me up when things get rough. Praise you that your truth trumps all the lies of the world. Amen.*

I WANT TO BE
RECOGNIZED

Matthew 7:16 "By their fruit you will recognize them."

How do you recognize a runner? On race days it's obvious who the runners are. Everywhere you look a sea of people stretching out, bold bib numbers pinned on their shirts. Yes, it's a dead giveaway! They must be runners.

Driving through a popular park, you can easily identify the runners. People of all ages clothed with running attire. Pounding the pavement, they stay within the lined paths marked out just for them. It'd be pretty hard not to notice who the runners are in that setting.

What if you walked into a running store? Wouldn't you assume the customers in there were runners shopping for the latest running apparel? Sure! You'd expect to find runners in a running store.

The car in front of you displays bumper magnets with the numbers 13.1 or 26.2. Doesn't this declare to all motorists that a runner is on board?

But aside from these *familiar* scenarios, how do people recognize runners?

Standing in line at a coffee shop, you might overhear a conversation between two people behind you.

"I'm registered for the 5K coming up next month! Are you running it this year?"

"Yeah, it's a really great course. Hope my pace is faster than last year."

These two people aren't dressed in running attire, but you gather from their *conversation* that they are indeed runners, passionate for their upcoming race.

While driving through a downpour, you spot a figure in the distance moving slowly. Upon closer evaluation it appears to be a runner soaked to the bone, perseverance written all over her face. This is most certainly a *serious runner* and not just someone taking a leisurely stroll.

How do you identify another Christian? If you walked into a church building, you'd be surrounded by them. You'd assume that the majority of the people were Christians.

If you entered a Christian bookstore, you'd observe patrons browsing shelves for Bibles and books written by Christian authors. Wouldn't you expect to find Christians in a place like this? But step *outside* the walls of church buildings and religious businesses. How does the world recognize Christians?

Maybe they see scripture inscribed on tee-shirts. The name of Jesus proclaimed on bumper stickers. Christian symbols plastered across social media. These are positive things declaring our faith. But if this is the *only evidence* identifying us as Christians to the world, something is wrong.

In today's verse (Matthew 7:16), Jesus states that his followers will be recognized *by their fruit.* What fruit stands out, letting you know someone is a follower of Christ? Maybe you see someone praying at a restaurant before eating their meal. You observe someone responding with gentleness instead of criticism to a cranky server at a busy restaurant.

When someone is trudging through a downpour of awful circumstances, you don't hear them complaining full of bitterness.

Instead, you see them walking through life with grace and perseverance, sharing their faith with others.

If people around us didn't know we attended church or Christian events, would they recognize us as Christians? What evidence could they point to? When they hear our conversations, does anything stand out? Do our attitudes passionately display the fruits of the spirit or do we blend in with the world? When life throws us challenging circumstances, what are we characterized by—grumbling or grace?

Our outward attire leads others to conclude we're runners. In the same way, our compassion and kindness should speak loud and clear. Our humility, gentleness, and patience should draw others in. Above all, our love should convince others we belong to Jesus.

READY? Can you identify a time you noticed a stranger whose behavior persuaded you they must be a Christian? Which fruits of the spirit do you think others recognize in your own life? Are your conversations and responses to challenges characterized by grumbling or grace?

GET SET. John 13:35 "By this everyone will know that you are my disciples, if you love one another." (Also read Colossians 3:12)

GO! *Lord Jesus, I pray for the Holy Spirit to lead me in all things so that others will see the fruit in my life, pointing them to you. Let your love flow freely through me so others will know I belong to you. Amen.*

HITTING THE WALL

Psalm 18:29 "In your strength I can crush an army; with my God I can scale any wall."

Labored breathing ignites. Weakness spreads through your body. Sore muscles ache with intense pain. Exhaustion soaks up the last drops of motivation. Overwhelmed with the miles left to go, your pace slows down to a shuffle. Negative thoughts saturate your mind. *Impossible. I can't keep going.*

You've hit the wall. Sometimes without warning, it's when sudden fatigue and loss of energy overtake us runners. Some have described hitting the wall like this: *A sledgehammer slammed down on my entire body. A charging elephant trampled me to the ground. My legs turned into concrete.*

Once you've hit a wall, you must embrace some proven strategies to keep going. Slow down your pace and walk. Stretch out your achy muscles. Consume a sports drink or gel to refuel. Whatever you do, don't just stop. As impossible as it seems, keep putting one foot in front of the other. Break up your remaining distance into segments. Tell yourself you're going to make it to the next mile marker, streetlight, intersection, or building. Luis Manzo, a sports psychologist and running coach, recommends recruiting a running partner to jump in with you at a point where you anticipate a struggle in the run, almost as if fighting *for you*.[6]

After years in the wilderness, Joshua and the Israelites came face-to-face with *their* wall. The city of Jericho, surrounded by walls twelve feet high and five feet thick, stopped them in their tracks. It looked impossible. Insurmountable. Thoughts of giving up and turning around flooded their minds. Yet God led them—through Joshua—to courageously conquer what appeared impossible. They were instructed to march around the city walls one time for six days in a row. It probably didn't make sense to them. But they kept marching, one step at a time. Finally on the seventh day, God told Joshua to have the people march around seven times! Imagine being in that crowd of people. Exhausted. Nothing left. Feeling stuck. In that moment they could've walked away and given up hope. Yet they kept on going. Faithfully moving forward one step at a time. And there in front of their very eyes they watched those seemingly impenetrable walls come crashing down. (Joshua 6:2—16)

In our own lives, we sometimes feel like we've hit a wall. We come face-to-face with something that stops us in our tracks, knocking us off our feet. Suddenly crushed to the core, negative thoughts flood our mind. *I'm done! I can't get through this!*

What's a real-life wall look like? A troubled marriage. Poor health diagnosis. Losing your job. Financial distress. A strained relationship. Your wall may look totally different, though, but it's anything that appears *impossible* or *insurmountable*. Whatever it is, there is hope. No matter how wide or how tall your wall looks, it's not the end.

When we focus on the actual wall in front of us, despair and fear overwhelm us. But God promises to go ahead of us, making our path straight. Just like the Israelites, we can trust God's unique plan even when it doesn't make sense. We keep moving, one foot in front of the other. We don't run in the opposite direction. We don't stand still as if paralyzed. We persevere and keep going. We let God do the fighting *for us.*

READY? Identify a wall you're facing right now. Are you standing still or running away from it? What's the next step you can take to get through the wall? Are you willing to keep going even when God's plan doesn't make sense?

GET SET. Hebrews 11:30 "It was by faith that the people of Israel marched around Jericho for seven days, and the walls came crashing down." (Also read Joshua 6:2–16)

GO! *Dear God, I thank you for your faithfulness and patience with me when I'm facing a wall in my life. Help me focus on your truth and strength instead of the obstacles in front of me. Help me walk obediently with confidence, just as the Israelites did when Joshua led them around the city walls. Amen.*

BLIND FAITH

Psalm 32:8 "I will instruct you and teach you in the way you should go; I will guide you with my eye upon you."

Just five more minutes and the race would start. Runners all around me jogged in place to stay warm, setting stopwatches, taking start-line photos, and stretching one last time. My GPS watch was set. My eyes fixed ahead. Suddenly some runners to my left brushed up against me. I glanced over and noticed a young man with a rope tied to his waist. An older man in front of him tightly held the other end of the rope in his hand. The older man sported a bright-orange vest with the word *Guide* boldly printed on the back. It was obvious the young man was blind. And he wasn't a spectator ... *he was going to run the race*. Wow! I couldn't believe this man was going to run a half-marathon ... blind. He was completely at the mercy of his guide.

I avoid obstacles when I run. Patches of ice, cracked sidewalks, uneven pathways, and scattered debris cause interference if you're not watching closely. Sometimes other people get in the way as I'm trying to maneuver around them. But I have *perfect vision*! I can see where the road gets narrow or where an incline is waiting for me to push harder. Can you imagine running any distance blind? You'd have to possess a strong *trust* in the person guiding you to let them lead you like that.

Oh, to have this kind of faith in our journey of life—with God as *our* guide! The kind of faith that doesn't doubt. The kind of faith that trusts completely. The kind of faith that says *"Okay, God, I can't see what's up ahead, but I trust you to lead me through this challenge.* So often we're guilty of untying the rope that connects us to God and decide to do things our own way. Thinking we know better and don't need his help, we let go of the rope. Then we wonder later how we got off track and why we crashed and burned from something we didn't see before. Why do we doubt? Why don't we trust?

The blind runner wasn't anxious. His beaming smile spoke volumes. Maybe he felt secure because he was firmly attached to his guide. The writer in today's verse confidently states that God's watchful eye is on us as he guides us (Psalm 32:8). Perhaps that's the key to our security in God: to be firmly attached to him. That means we fix our eyes on him. We seek him wholeheartedly. We stay as close to him as we can possibly get. If we truly do this, maybe we won't be anxious. Then we can display a beaming smile for all around us to see. And when people are attracted to our joyous countenance, we can point them to our awesome guide.

Wherever you are, I encourage you to hold tightly to God. Whatever your struggle, he will show you the next step. Stay close to him because he knows what's up ahead. It might not be easy, but he promises to be with you every step of the way.

READY? Is your rope tied tightly to your heavenly guide? Or is it starting to lose its grip? Do you trust God to help you navigate the unknown road up ahead? Can you identify times when you've let go of the rope? What were the consequences of letting go? Keep your rope tightly tied and stay close to your Savior.

GET SET. Psalm 25:4–6 "Show me your ways, O Lord, teach me your paths; guide me in your truth and teach me, for you are God my Savior, and my hope is in you all day long."

GO! *Lord God, I ask you to secure my rope tightly to your side. Help me keep it firmly tied and not be tempted to loosen its grip. I confess the times I've chosen my own way. Forgive my unbelief! Help me trust you when I can't see what's up ahead. Help me rest securely in the fact that you are in control and you know what's best for me. Thank you for directing my steps. Thank you for the hope you've promised. Amen.*

FIGURING OUT
YOUR COURSE

**Jeremiah 29:11 "For I know the plans I have for you,"
declares the Lord, "plans to prosper you and not to harm you,
plans to give you hope and a future."**

For most official races, runners can view the course online.
You can view every single twist and turn. In detail, you can see
the highest point of elevation. You know precisely at which mile
markers the path will ascend to steep hills. You can sigh with
relief knowing exactly where the path will descend, giving you
breaks throughout the race. Some runners will even determine
whether or not to register for a race based on the course layout.
*Too many hills! I want a flatter course. Better not run this race, the
elevation is too steep towards the end. I'll be too exhausted.*

You can even view the places where water stops are located.
Knowing this beforehand, runners can train to run specific
lengths, spacing out their water intake. Mentally you can prepare
for worst-case scenarios, seeing exactly where medical tents are
located. Most importantly, you can see exactly where the finish

line is. You tuck the names of the intersecting streets in the back of your mind. *That's where I'll finish the race. That's where my family will meet me afterwards and congratulate me.*

All of this information we are privy to is great! Can you imagine how cool it would be to see the course of your *real life*? To actually see in detail what would be in your future? You'd see every exciting milestone awaiting you. In wonderful elation, you'd anticipate all those mountaintop experiences in your future.

But if you examined the course a little closer, you'd also see the dark valleys up ahead. *What?!* Just around that corner you'd see a marriage crumbling, ending in divorce. The unexpected job loss—the one you thought was secure just a few miles back. *Huh?!* And if you kept looking further down the course, you'd find that one of your kids has broken your heart. And you don't even see a medical tent anywhere in sight. What would you do?

Maybe you wouldn't even want to continue your race of life any longer. *I can't bear the thought of these things coming. I want an easier course. I won't be able to live this kind of life.*

Thankfully, we don't get this kind of information in our journey of life. That's not how God designed us to live. While we don't get to see the whole course of our lives mapped out in front of us, God does. We don't know the details of trials and challenges headed our way, but he does. We can't fathom the abundant blessings he has in store for us, but he knows and can't wait to lavish them upon us. He's designed us to live one moment at a time, in total dependence on him. Our flesh craves to see an entire mile at a time. But the Holy Spirit wants to lead us one *step* at a time. Our flesh wants to know how long a certain trial will last. But the Holy Spirit wants us to trust.

When we register to run the race of faith with Jesus as our guide, we run with all our might. We run with boldness and perseverance. We run like there's no tomorrow. In fact, we don't know what a day will bring forth. We may think our course is quite long, but we don't know exactly where our finish line will be. Whether it's a quick 5K or multiple marathons back-to-back, we must keep on running. Keep on trusting. Keep on thriving. So while we don't know *where* our earthly finish line will be, we know *who* is leading us on the course. And we are promised that he will greet us at the intersection of time and eternity. Now *that's* something to get excited about!

READY? If there were one thing you could figure out about your future, what would it be? Are you willing to surrender this concern to Jesus? Take some extended time to pray about your fears and worries and lay them at the foot of the cross.

GET SET. Proverbs 16:9 "A man's heart plans his way, but the Lord determines his steps."

GO! *Lord Jesus, help me to trust you with every twist and turn of my life. I'm so prone to worry and wanting to know what's up ahead that I'm missing out on knowing you more intimately. Help me to let go of the things out of my control and trust you completely. Amen.*

WHAT'S YOUR TRAINING PLAN?

Psalm 119:105 "Your word is a lamp for my feet, a light for my path."

Monday – short run. Tuesday – strength training. Wednesday – cross training. Thursday – short run. Friday – strength training. Saturday – long run. Sunday – rest!

Are you following a training plan? Whether you're a beginning runner or a seasoned veteran with a wall of medals, you've got to have a plan. You need to know what your strategy is from day-to-day in preparation for upcoming races.

Training plans are usually developed by experts. They develop plans so runners will develop endurance to successfully complete whatever their distance goals may be. Many faithfully follow Jeff Galloway's trademark plan, designed for those who desire a mix of running and walking. Running expert Hal Higdon is known for his myriad of training plans for every running level.

Once you embrace a specific training plan, you know without a doubt that it's equipping you to be a better runner. And most importantly, it enables you to cross the finish line.

Imagine a half marathon on the horizon without a training plan in place. Would you just go with the flow from week to week depending on how you felt? Would you show up at the start line unprepared?

Just as runners follow a training plan, we follow a training plan to live our lives for Christ. In this case, there's not a multitude of plans to choose from. It's called the Bible. Whether you're a new Christian learning to walk or a seasoned follower teaching others, we all live by this training manual. God's breathed, inspired, and flawless word. Not the opinion of men or current culture. This is what drives us. This is what aligns us with our creator. This is what keeps us on the righteous path. Without it, we're like a clueless runner with no training plan.

The Bible—our training manual for life—was developed by an expert. God himself used many people—led by the Holy Spirit—to write his story for us. From the creation to the fall, from the cross to redemption, he shows us who he is and how we are to live for him.

A runner's training plan dictates daily steps to accomplish. But when it comes to God's word, we have to dig a little deeper to hear him. We have to be still long enough to know what our next step is. We must be patient to study and soak up what God wants to show us. The word of God will challenge us, yet comfort us at the same time. The word of God will show us our sin up close, yet it equips us with strength. Whatever each day brings, God desires to teach, direct, and guide us on the path he's prepared for us.

When we embrace God's word, it equips us to be better followers of Christ. Whatever situations we face, his word gives us direction and insight. The strength we gain from the word of God enables us to thrive and not just survive. A finish line awaits us at the end of our earthly days. I don't know about you, but I want to arrive and hear him say, *"Well done, good and faithful servant."*

READY? How would your life change if you engaged in God's word with the same devotion you give your training plan for running?

Identify an area of your life where you need direction. Pray and ask God to speak to you through his word and show you your next step.

GET SET. 2 Timothy 3:16-17 "All scripture is God-breathed and is useful for teaching, rebuking, correcting and training in righteousness, so that the servant of God may be thoroughly equipped for every good work."

GO! *Heavenly Father, thank you for giving us your word! Please help me embrace it for every situation in my life. Help me to understand your word when it seems confusing. May your word guide and direct me for all my days no matter what others around me are saying. Amen.*

POUNDING THE PAVEMENT ALONE

Matthew 14:23 "After he had dismissed them, Jesus went up on a mountainside by himself to pray. Later that night, he was there alone."

Many runners prefer running with a group. Some won't budge without their best running buddy. Don't misunderstand: we all need the accountability and motivation other runners contribute. And there's nothing better in the world than having a best friend who runs your exact pace and rises early *with you*, encouraging you from start to finish.

But sometimes you'll have to run alone. Yikes! *But I can't. It's boring. I can't do it without someone beside me.* Ever hear yourself spouting off these words? Sometimes life brings uncontrollable circumstances. Sometimes our perfectly laid out buddy-running plan goes awry. Others will let us down when we least expect it.

Snow and ice prevent us from meeting our group at the park. Your running buddy hates rain and doesn't show up. Your running group leaves you behind while you attend to a sick child at home. Whatever the circumstances, you're left with a decision: either run alone or don't run at all. Running alone might mean wiping the dust off your treadmill in the basement. It might mean running solo at the park ... in the rain. Maybe you run in the blazing heat instead of the cool morning.

This is where the rubber hits the road. Just how serious are you to stay on track? How far will you go to be prepared? Yes. Sometimes you simply have to run alone. Without the chatter of others around you. Without the listening ear of your best friend.

Christ followers must sometimes make a similar decision. Sometimes we have to walk part of the journey alone. Now of course we aren't *really* alone. We know Jesus never leaves us. The Holy Spirit continually guides us. But sometimes we don't have other people walking with us. Maybe you've said the following: *I'm not going to church unless she goes with me. I'm not going to that Bible study unless my friends go with me. I can't sit by myself in the church service.*

But the reality is that sometimes things happen beyond our control. Your friend drops out of church for a while. Your work schedule is changed, keeping you from continuing your small group Bible study. Sickness keeps you homebound, leaving you unable to get to church. Whatever the case may be, you have to decide. Will you keep embracing Jesus even if you have to walk some steps alone? Walking alone might mean opening up your Bible by yourself at the coffee shop. Perhaps you embrace solitude for a season until you find another small group. It might mean you have an extended season of quiet searching while you heal from sickness.

God called Moses on a solo journey for forty days—away from the crowd (Exodus 24). Daniel knew what it felt like to walk alone. When he resolved to keep praying no matter what the law said, he ended up in the lion's den *by himself* (Daniel 6). David faced Goliath *alone* while the entire Israelite army cowered in fear (1 Samuel 17). Old Testament prophets Jeremiah and Isaiah would've made great running buddies, but God called each to walk *alone*, proclaiming the truth (Jeremiah 1, Isaiah 6).

Jesus modeled for us what it means to walk alone. Crowds traveled with him. The twelve disciples followed him. John remained faithful to him. But multiple times he got up early while it was still dark and went out *alone* to pray. Even when he pleaded with his closest friends to pray with him, they let him down. Yet he still showed up and fulfilled his purpose!

READY? Can you identify a season in your life when you had to walk alone? How did this affect your faith? What are some blessings in disguise that come from sometimes walking alone? If you're in one of those seasons now, admit your fears and worries and lay them at the feet of Jesus.

GET SET. Exodus 24:2 "Moses alone is to approach the Lord; the others must not come near."

GO! *Heavenly Father, I thank you for the promise that you'll never leave me or forsake me. Help my faith to grow strong and go deep when I must walk parts of my life journey alone. I trust you to bring others into my life for support and encouragement at the right time. Amen.*

THE HALFWAY POINT

Nehemiah 4:6 "So we rebuilt the wall until all of it reached half its height, for the people worked with all their heart."

One and a half miles. You're halfway through a 5K. Just a little bit past a 5K, you're halfway through a 10K. At 6.5 you've hit the halfway point of a half-marathon. And for those who are determined enough to run a full marathon, 13.1 miles is your halfway mark.

Halfway.

Some runners view the halfway point as major progress. Excitement oozes out through pouring sweat. Reaching this place in any race—no matter what the distance—ushers in mixed thoughts and emotions. *Look how far I've come! I'm halfway through! The hardest part is over.*

But others might see the halfway point with a completely different perspective. *I'm only halfway through? I can't possibly repeat the same distance I've just come. I thought I was closer to the finish line. I thought my pace would be quicker than this.*

In 2009, Jenny Barringer was favored to win the NCAA cross country championship race. At first, Jenny confidently held the lead. Surely she'd win the coveted first place title. But midway through the race, something happened. Jenny's pace slowed considerably. Runners who trailed her suddenly whizzed past, leaving Jenny gasping for breath. She dropped to tenth place, then twentieth. Struggling to keep up, she later crossed the finish line in 169th place. When questioned after the race, Jenny explained, "Halfway into it, I didn't feel so good. It was sudden. I thought I couldn't run." It wasn't an injury that slowed her down. *It was her perception.* Discouraging thoughts paralyzed her, leading to utter panic.[7]

In the Old Testament we find the prophet Nehemiah at a crucial turning point. He'd reached the halfway mark in rebuilding Jerusalem's broken walls. Compelled with undertaking this impossible task, the odds were against him. He courageously led the Jewish people for twenty-six straight days in an ultra building project (Nehemiah 2—4). That's when their enemies started taunting and threatening them. Halfway through, a choice had to be made. Allow the enemies of criticism and discouragement to halt their efforts, or keep persevering in spite of how they perceived the remaining work?

In the same way, we too approach halfway points in our lives. We're midway through a tough project at school or work. Halfway through a challenging phase in our child's development. Maybe it's the halfway point of a business venture, ministry dream, or a recovery period in our health. Whatever our halfway point is, our perception of it determines the outcome.

So how did Nehemiah proceed? He chose to embrace faith in God instead of letting discouragement and defeat rule over him. He challenged the people with these powerful words: "Do not be afraid of them. Remember the Lord, great and awesome (Nehemiah 4:14)." He chose to help put their mind in the right perspective. He reminded them there was no reason for fear. Greater was he who was in them than he who was in the world. The opposite of discouragement is faith. While discouragement looks for and believes the worst, faith believes God and his promises.

READY? Identify a time in your life when you reached a halfway point. How did you proceed? How did your perception affect the outcome? Are you approaching or standing at a halfway point now? Resolve to embrace truth and faith instead of discouragement and defeat.

GET SET. Deuteronomy 31:8 "It is the Lord who goes before you. He will be with you; he will not leave you or forsake you. Do not fear or be dismayed."

GO! *Lord Jesus, when I find myself at a halfway point, please give me your eyes. May I not give in to discouragement in those moments. Help me embrace your truth and trust you. Give me a heart of faith that will keep me strong for your glory. Amen.*

WATCH OUT FOR BLACK ICE

Proverbs 16:18 "Pride goes before destruction, a haughty spirit before a fall."

Surrounded by a winter wonderland, my running group prepared to take off on our weekly long run. Three inches of snow had fallen just days before. Previously covered roads were now cleared completely ... or so it seemed. We were warned to look out for black ice before heading out for our six-mile run. Mounds of snow lined the edges of the road. The path ahead *looked* safe, yet patches of black ice couldn't be detected with the naked eye.

A few runners in front of me plodded in their perfect stride, their eyes fixed ahead. Suddenly one of them slipped! She tried furiously to catch herself, but her attempt proved futile. Bam! Spinning out of control, she tumbled onto the frozen ground. Shaken, she slowly stood up, caught her breath, and continued—at a much slower pace. Nobody could see the culprit—that sneaky patch of black ice lurching in the shadows. She didn't realize its presence until it was too late.

Black ice. Why is it called this? If it were *black*, wouldn't one be able to see it? But by definition, black ice refers to a thin coating of glazed ice on a surface. Because of its transparency, it allows black asphalt roadways to be seen *through* it. It's practically invisible to drivers as well as runners, causing a risk of skidding and accidents due to the loss of traction.

Isn't black ice kind of like those sins we hold onto sometimes? Not the outward ones obvious to most. No, I'm referring to the ones that are embedded *deep within us*. Those secret sins we try to keep hidden. To the naked eye, they can't be detected. On the outside we may look polished, presentable, and perfect, but deep inside there's a losing battle with an ugly thing called *pride*. Although it can't be seen, pride will rear its ugly head out of nowhere when least expected and before we know it, we're sliding. Skidding. Losing our balance. We try with all our human might to catch ourselves, just like the runner I witnessed. But most often we come to an abrupt halt and crash humbly to the ground.

Today's scripture gives us a stern warning. Pride comes before a fall (Proverbs 16:18). Just when we think we've paced ourselves with our perfect stride, patting ourselves on the back for all we think we've done in our own power, that's when we're most susceptible to the black ice of pride.

I'm not like that person. I'm better than he is. I haven't given in to the sin she struggles with. I've got this—I don't need any help.

We blow ourselves up with such powerful pride that we don't even see the ground beneath us. We don't see the danger of what's ahead. Pride is such a deadly sin because it takes our eyes off Jesus and puts the focus on self. Instead of going at the pace designed for us, we do things our own way and suddenly we lose traction, falling to the ground.

READY? Do you ever find yourself pointing out obvious sins of others? Why are we so quick to do so? Are there areas of your own life where God is pointing out pride? Are you willing to humble yourself and surrender before you fall? Ask him to shine his light on your pride.

GET SET. Proverbs 11:12 "When pride comes, then comes disgrace, but with humility comes wisdom." (Also read Proverbs 29:23)

GO! *Heavenly Father, please forgive me for the times I've judged others for outward sins when I've neglected to see the pride in my own heart. Help me keep my eyes on you one step at a time so I can be aware of anything that would cause me to fall. Thank you for your grace. Amen.*

DON'T GET DISQUALIFIED

2 Timothy 2:5 "If anyone competes as an athlete, he does not receive the victor's crown unless he competes according to the rules."

In 1980, Rosie Ruiz crossed the finish line of the Boston Marathon in a world-record pace. However, it was soon discovered that she'd cheated. No wonder her time appeared suspicious. She'd taken the subway towards the end of the course! Her scheming ended in disqualification. No medal. Barred from future races, her name would never appear on the winner's list.[8]

Unfortunately, she's not the only one guilty of cutting corners. Every year it is estimated that almost 400 people are disqualified from the four most popular marathons due to *cheating*. Some runners give their bib numbers to faster runners during a race and end up with medals in their age brackets. Some take shortcuts by stepping off the course and rejoining it closer to the finish line, cutting off several miles.[9]

So it really doesn't matter how quick your pace is. It doesn't matter how well-known you are. And your track record alone means nothing. If you don't compete according to the rules of the race, you'll be disqualified.

Just as weary marathon runners are tempted to take shortcuts at a crucial turning point in the race, we as Christians can be tempted to take shortcuts on our journey of faith. We might have a pretty good track record and considered a strong Christian, but sometimes the temptations are incredibly strong and, before we know it, we've gone our own way, thinking it will be okay in the long run. God has lovingly designed his world with boundaries—rules for our own good. Rules that don't mix well with shortcuts. What would some shortcuts look like in our lives today?

Fudging the expense reports. Lying to our neighbor. Overlooking our children's foolish behavior because we're too tired. Skipping worship to sleep in. Keeping our tithe to have more money for vacation. Refusing to apologize to someone we've offended. Clicking on that website we know will take us down a wrong path. These are just a few examples of shortcuts we might be tempted to take along the way.

None of us are exempt from temptation. We are faced all the time with choices to take shortcuts. We're all susceptible. Even the apostle Paul—with the stellar track record he had—was aware of his ability to fall. He continued to discipline his soul, being careful not to become disqualified himself. He was careful to not let pride sneak in and trip him up. And he exhorts us to do the same (1 Corinthians 9:24—27). Being disqualified spiritually doesn't mean we're exempt from our home in Heaven, but some interpret this to mean that if we become *characterized* at cutting corners, we can't be used efficiently for spreading the gospel message to others. We'd be guilty of causing others to stumble if they followed us on our path to a shortcut.

Imagine a crowd of runners trailing behind the woman who cheated in the marathon. Perhaps they would simply follow her because they thought she was an excellent runner who knew the way. Identify a shortcut you've taken in your own life and imagine if others followed your lead. It makes us ponder whether or not we are being good stewards of the gospel message. Although we're going to sin, we don't have to choose to be disqualified from being used in God's kingdom. Staying humble and embracing the boundaries God has put into place will keep us running our races more effectively.

READY? Think back to a time in your life where you gave in to the shortcut of temptation. How did it turn out? What temptation(s) are you facing now? What can you do today to stay on course?

GET SET. 1 Corinthians 9:27 "No, I strike a blow to my body and make it my slave so that after I have preached to others, I myself will not be disqualified for the prize."

GO! *Dear God, thank you for the reminder of what can happen when we choose ways outside of yours. Help me to grasp the truth that you truly have our best interests at heart. Help me when I am tempted to do things my way. Help me be a faithful steward of the gospel you've entrusted to me for your kingdom. Amen.*

WHICH SIDE ARE YOU RUNNING ON?

Romans 12:2 "Do not conform any longer to the pattern of this world but be transformed by the renewing of you mind."

Cars approaching you closer and closer. Zooming past you, just inches away. It's enough to usher in a wave of fear, making you wonder if you'll get plowed over. It can feel downright awkward and vulnerable. This just seems backward. You feel like every driver is staring you down. For safety, runners are urged to run on the left side of the road—facing traffic. Huh? It doesn't make sense! It would feel much more comfortable to run *with* the flow of traffic rather than against it.

The truth is you're doing the right thing by running *against* traffic. Running on the left shoulder facing oncoming traffic is much safer than having cars at your back. In most states, it's not even a matter of choice: the law requires that runners face oncoming traffic. Oncoming traffic can better see you. If you ran on the right side of the road, you couldn't see what's coming *behind* you. Distracted drivers (texting or looking at their phones) won't be able to see you until the last minute. Or in some cases, won't see you at all until it's too late.

Runners who run *with* traffic are dangerously putting themselves at high risk. So the best way to prevent an untimely meeting with a vehicle is to be able to *see* them. And that means you must run against the traffic and ignore what appears to be a comfortable pattern.

As followers of Christ, we are called to stand out from the world. We are set apart. That means we don't conform to the ways of our culture. The spirit of this world opposes the ways of God. The spirit of this world is wrapped around pleasing self. People who are not God-driven are caught up in the whirlwind of a dangerous traffic pattern. Its force is strong. At times it may even look appealing, beckoning us to join in. If we aren't careful, we can get distracted. Before we know it, we're caught up in the rushing current of sin. And then we think it's no big deal because everyone's doing it. *This is the path everyone is traveling, so it must be right.*

Just as runners go against the flow of traffic for physical safety, we must resolve to walk the narrow path for the life of our soul. As tempting as it may be to blend in with the world, we must commit our lives to walk as Jesus did. We must embrace the path he has laid out for us. This path will not look like that of our unbelieving neighbors and coworkers. This path will not be popular. This path will not *feel* comfortable. On the contrary, this path will feel awkward. It will cause us to feel very vulnerable before others. Walking this path will go against every fleshly desire welling up inside us. But this is the path we must embrace if we are true followers of Christ.

Hurting people in this world will notice us plain as day. Broken hearts will be drawn to the hope radiating out of us. Empty souls will turn in our direction, longing to be filled. But they won't notice us if we're blending in with the traffic pattern of the world.

READY? As a follower of Christ, which side of the road are you running on? When are you tempted to blend in with the world? What is your response when it feels everything is against you?

What steps can you take to confidently run your race of faith on the righteous path God has laid out?

GET SET. Proverbs 16:25 "There is a way that appears to be right, but in the end it leads to death."

GO! *Lord Jesus, this world is a tough place to live in. It's so easy to get caught up in the flow of what seems right. I desperately cry out and ask you to strengthen me. Help me to be brave and walk the path you've laid out for me. Help me be faithful even when it feels like everyone is against me. Amen.*

GET OUT OF YOUR COMFORT ZONE

Matthew 14:29–31 "So Peter got out of the boat. He walked on the water toward Jesus. But when Peter saw the wind, he was afraid. He began to sink. He cried out, 'Lord, save me!' Right away Jesus reached out His hand and caught him. 'Your faith is so small! Why did you doubt me?'"

After running six half marathons during a four-year stretch, I felt God nudging me to attempt a *full* marathon. At first I fought against this gentle nudging. *What? Are you getting me mixed up with someone else, God? Can't I just be a spectator in the crowd cheering for those crazy marathoners?* But when I realized he was indeed nudging me, I finally consented. Yep! I stepped *way* out of my comfort zone. I'd grown quite comfortable in running *half* marathons. I knew what to expect. I was comfortable with my pace. Comfortable with the training schedule. I'd grown confident with every attempt of beating my previous race times. My collection of half-marathon medals fully satisfied me.

But when I finally decided to give it a shot, I stepped into *unknown territory*. Several days passed before I mustered up enough courage to actually register for the race. And once I officially registered, fear gripped my heart. I was no longer comfortable.

Maybe you're comfortable jogging a few miles around the block, but you think you'd be too uncomfortable to actually sign up for a 5K. Perhaps you've grown accustomed to running nothing but 5K's and the mere thought of going beyond that makes you break out in a sweat. You don't want to leave your comfort zone because it's just not … comfortable. But you know what? Sometimes that's exactly where God wants us to be.

In today's passage, I'm sure Peter felt the same way. It's pretty obvious that he most certainly stepped out of *his* comfort zone! The disciples huddled together, watching *comfortably* from *inside* the boat. But then Peter took a leap of faith as he slowly slid his trembling feet over the edge of the boat. Nobody else dared to follow behind him. He progressed from the role of spectator to one of participant. Stepping completely out of the boat, he walked toward Jesus (Matthew 14:29—31).

Where in your life is Jesus calling you to stop watching and step out of your comfort zone? There's a time and place to watch from the sidelines until Jesus says it's time to become a participant. When Peter saw the huge waves in the distance, he began to sink. But he didn't sink because the wind and waves were *present*; he sank because he *took his eyes off Jesus*. When Jesus calls us out of our comfort zones, the wind and waves of this world threaten to take us down. What are they for you? Doubts from your inner soul? Criticism from others who don't understand? Unexpected circumstances?

When Peter began to sink, he didn't have to wait very long for Jesus to rescue him. It's because Jesus was right there! When Jesus calls you out of your comfort zone, he doesn't just watch from a distance. He is right there beside you, catching you when you fall. Even that first step into the unknown can bring you to your knees, but all you have to do is humbly ask him for help.

READY? Are you still in the boat? Then trust him as you take that first step out. Are you a few steps out of the boat? Then keep going one step at a time, fixing your eyes on Jesus. Are you beginning to sink? Then call out to him! He is waiting.

GET SET. Psalm 105:4 "Look to the Lord and his strength; seek his face always."

GO! *Lord Jesus, I humbly ask you to show me where I need to come out of my own comfort zone. Please forgive my unbelief and my human tendency to worry. May I not focus on the gushing waves around me, but on the strength and peace you promise when we seek your face. Amen.*

HEALING OUR INJURIES

Ezekiel 34:16 "I will bind up the injured and strengthen the weak...."

One day you're running your perfect pace. You feel like you're soaring above the entire world and nothing could stop you. Bam! Without warning, you feel a stabbing pain in your hamstring. You slow down hoping it's just a slight cramp, but as you continue on, you realize the hard truth: you've strained your muscle. With each step you wince in pain. How could this happen? Why now? Instead of continuing your run, you limp to your car. Waves of disappointment wash over you, and the next day you're sitting in the doctor's office.

The longer you continue running, it's likely you'll encounter an injury at some point. For some of us, it's major. A torn muscle. Excruciating knee pain. A sprained ankle. Even the minor injuries stop us in our tracks, putting us on the sidelines temporarily. If we keep going and ignore the pain, we'll only make it worse, causing further damage. We have to face the truth and get proper treatment, allowing our injuries to heal. Whether its surgery, physical therapy, or prolonged rest, we must accept the treatment plan advised. The hardest part is waiting. Waiting for the injury to heal. Waiting for the weak part of our body to become strong again.

In the same way and because we're human, it's certain we'll sustain injuries along the course of life. More often than not, these injuries come when we least expect them. Maybe we're thriving and feel as if nothing could stop us—living in our sweet spot. But one day without warning we're bombarded, sustaining a serious injury. One that knocks us off our feet, leaving us wounded with pain. But I'm not talking about a physical injury.

The most painful injuries are the ones that wound our *soul*. The kind that make you wonder how you'll ever take another step. The injuries that crush our spirit. Wounds from family members. Betrayals from friends. Disappointments in the workplace. Unthinkable tragedies.

If we keep going without addressing our wounded heart, more damage will surely be done. As deep as our pain may be, we must humbly admit we need help. As much as we want to thrive, we may be slowed down to simply *survive*. For a season, we hobble over to the sidelines and cry out to our Heavenly Father—the one who heals.

Because he heals in a variety of ways, his treatment plan is unique for each of us. If we listen closely, he will show us the next step in our healing. Maybe it's fellow believers walking alongside us for a season. Perhaps we slow down our busy schedule, embracing prolonged rest. In some cases we might seek professional help.

But one thing is for certain: there will be a period of waiting. Waiting for our wounded heart to heal. Waiting for the weakest part of our soul to be strengthened. But we don't have to wait alone. That's when our Heavenly Father does his best work. He specializes in healing our wounds. He delights in taking the damaged parts of our life, turning the broken pieces into something beautiful.

READY? Where in your life have you felt wounded? Have you taken steps to heal from your pain? If not, are you ready to ask God to show you what your next step is? Can you trust him with the treatment plan he recommends?

GET SET. Psalm 34:18 "God is near to the brokenhearted and saves those who are crushed in spirit." (Also read Psalm 27:14)

GO! *Heavenly Father, I am hurting from wounds in my heart. I bring these before you and ask you to strengthen and heal like only you can. It's so hard to wait because my flesh wants a quick fix. Help me to trust you as I wait. Amen.*

GLOW IN THE DARK

Philippians 2:14–16 "Do everything without grumbling or arguing, so that you may become blameless and pure, children of God without fault in a warped and crooked generation. Then you will shine among them like stars in the sky as you hold firmly to the word of life. And then I will be able to boast on the day of Christ that I did not run or labor in vain."

Pitch darkness. No light whatsoever. You can't see or be seen! But it's time to run. This is our reality when running before dawn or when daylight savings comes to an end. For many of us, the shorter days wreak havoc on our running schedules. Running in the dark poses a greater threat, forcing us to take precautions. According to the Governors Highway Safety Association, 70 percent of pedestrian deaths occur between 6:00 PM and 6:00 AM.[10] We have to be intentional, making ourselves visible to motorists. It's a matter of life and death.

There's an array of items available for protecting runners in the dark: headlamps, flashing strobe lights, and a myriad of reflective clothing. These essential items are designed to illuminate your path on darkened roads and improve visibility. It's amazing how a tiny light allows motorists to see you before dawn and after dusk.

Bringing up the rear in our group training run, I looked ahead in the pitch darkness. No sign of the sun. But I could still clearly see my buddy's flashing light up ahead. Like a bright star in the sky, it shone brightly, showing me where to go.

Just as runners attach lights to be seen in the dark, we must let God's light shine through us in the darkness of this world. We're told in today's key scripture to *hold firmly to the word of life*. The word of life is the gospel message of Jesus, revealing eternal life through him. He calls us to live in such a way that we stand out in a world full of people without hope (Philippians 2:14—16). The moral decline of our world is quickly accelerating. In a time when we're tempted to run away from the chaos around us, we're instead called to stand firm. Radiating the hope within us, we're like beacons of light.

The runner's headlamp illuminates her own path, but most importantly it allows others to *see her!* Once we have the hope of Jesus living in us, we must share that light with others who are still in darkness. There may be times when you see absolutely no light around you. All seems gloomy and bleak. You doubt if your life really matters. But it's time to keep running the race of faith. It's time to embrace Jesus and stay strong. It's a matter of life for the souls around you.

Running in the dark means one must be intentional in choosing reflective gear. In the same way, we can only reflect the light of Jesus to others if we're intentional in choosing the path he's called us to. If there's ever been a time for embracing the truth and power of Jesus, it is now. To know him and make him known—this is the calling of everyone who claims to follow him.

READY? Can you identify an area of darkness in your own life? Are you willing to let Jesus shine his light there? Where do you sense Jesus calling you to shine his light to others around you who need the message of hope?

‹ LISA PREUETT ›

GET SET. John 8:12 "Jesus spoke to them, saying, 'I am the light of the world. Whoever follows me will not walk in darkness, but will have the light of life.'" (Also read 2 Corinthians 4:6)

GO! *Lord Jesus, praise your holy name that there is no place too dark for your light to shine. Help me surrender to the light you want to shine through me so others can see your glory and power. Give me strength and wisdom for living a life pleasing to you in a world where there is much darkness. Amen.*

‹ 115 ›

WHO ARE YOU COMPETING AGAINST?

2 Corinthians 10:12 "When they measure themselves by themselves and compare themselves with themselves, they are not wise."

Just a few hours after the 10K, the race results glared on the screen in front of me. Every single person who finished the race could be searched—from the winner all the way to the last person who crossed the finish line. Plugging in my name, I viewed my results. There in front of me I could see my total time and average pace.

Just as I was starting to feel good about my accomplishment, I looked at the next column over and saw another set of numbers: number in age group, my placement in that specific age group, my placement in the entire race. A lot of other women in my age bracket finished sooner than I did! Now I didn't feel so good about my time. *Shouldn't I be able to run at a faster pace like these women my same age?* Feelings of defeat washed over me.

To make myself feel better, I searched the results of women twenty years older than me. Now as I scrolled through finish times longer than mine, I felt a sense of pride. *Well, at least I beat these women. I didn't come in last place.*

Unless we're the first one to cross the finish line, there will always be someone faster than us. But if we focus on *comparing* ourselves to others, we'll be left with disappointment. The opposite is true as well. If we compare ourselves with slower runners—just to feel better about ourselves—pride oozes out, breeding a false sense of security.

In the same manner, we sometimes mimic this behavior in other areas of our life. When we compare ourselves to people who are older, wiser, and richer, we find ourselves feeling defeated. *I should be further along, like her.* Before we know it, we continue the comparison game. To brush off these feelings, we turn our attention to those whom we feel are beneath us. Those who may be struggling in areas we are strong in. Those who are just beginning a journey we've already finished.

Oh, how foolish we are to do both of these! Gazing at others ahead of us—through the lens of comparison—leaves us discontent. Looking at those who are struggling—through a lens of judgment— leaves us prideful. Instead of comparing, shouldn't we focus on where *we are*? Shouldn't we strive to live the life God has called us to using the gifts and talents he's blessed us with to fulfill our purpose—instead of comparing them to others?

When we stand before God one day, we won't be standing beside anyone else. Each one of us must give an account for the life we lived. God won't scroll through a list of people and say, *Look, you should've done better than her.* And he won't say, *Great job, you performed better than these other people.*

Most runners embrace a PR approach in races. Personal Record. Instead of comparing our finish time with other *runners,* we compare our finish time to our own time in a *previous race.* We attempt to beat our best time. The person we aim to compete with is *ourselves.*

Maybe that's how we should approach our journey of faith. Instead of comparing our lives to others, we focus on making progress with our own struggles. Instead of judging others, we embrace humility, thanking God for rescuing us from our previous ways of sin. And when we conquer one area of sin, he takes us further and shows us something else.

READY? Have you ever compared yourself to other runners? Identify another area where you compare yourself to others. What effect does this have on you? Do you struggle more with discontentment or pride? Where does God want you to focus your attention?

GET SET. Galatians 6:4 "Each one should test their own actions. Then they can take pride in themselves alone, without comparing themselves to someone else."

GO! *Heavenly Father, forgive me for the times I've foolishly compared myself to others. Free me from any chains of discontentment or pride. Give me direction to focus on the life you've given me. Help me walk in humility. Give me victory over the sins I struggle with. Amen.*

THE BEST SIGN EVER

1 Corinthians 2:5 "That your faith might not rest in the wisdom of men but in the power of God."

From 5K's to full marathons, you can't go too far before crazy, colorful signs come into view. Bright, bold words splashed onto poster boards grab your attention. Many runners swear these signs have spurred them on at crucial points in a race. Those cheering us on have invented some creative signs over the years. Some of these signs will make you smile—maybe even get you to laugh out loud. Perhaps you've seen these among your favorites:

Run like you stole something.
Humpty Dumpty had wall issues too.
This seems like a lot of work for a free banana.
I'm sure it seemed like a good idea four months ago.
Hurry up Mom, we're hungry for lunch.

And then there are signs that shout out powerful truths, motivating you to keep going:

Don't stop, people are watching.
Forward is a pace.
The voice in your head that says you can't do this is a liar.
Focus on how far you've run instead of how far you have to go.
Pain is temporary, glory is forever.

When we're at crucial turning points in our lives, what kind of words motivate us to keep going? Is it people's opinions? Political slogans? Bumper stickers? What is it that will truly grab your heart and motivate you to keep running your race of faith?

Imagine some of the twelve disciples running a race. What would Jesus write on their signs to keep them going?

You're the Rock! Don't back down. (Peter)
I love you dearly. Don't stop. (John)
Believe Me! I'm here for you. (Thomas)

If Jesus were standing on the sideline among the crowd, what would his sign say specifically to *you*?

Don't listen to their criticism, I am with you.
Be courageous. I've designed you for this purpose.
Keep going, I promise you'll get through this.
You can't imagine what's waiting for you at the finish line.

I've seen my share of motivational posters on the sidelines. But one of my favorites is one that says **Touch here for power**. And right in the middle of this sign a colorful star is plastered. I've witnessed runners intentionally darting towards this sign, slapping the star with determination, believing this act will somehow give them a boost. I've done this myself! As silly as it sounds, touching the star on this sign brings a smile to my face.

Just for a moment, envision Jesus standing on the sideline, holding up this sign for all to see: **Touch here for power**. But there's no star next to these words. He is simply saying, "Come to me. The power you need *comes from me*."

We read about a desperate woman in the New Testament who purposely pushed her way through the crowd to touch Jesus. She needed physical healing and Jesus was her only hope. Reaching with all her might, her weary fingers pressed against him. In that exact moment Jesus said, "Someone touched me. I was aware that power had gone out of me." (Luke 8:43—48)

Here's the riveting truth, dear friends: Jesus is not standing on the sideline of your life with a written sign. He's running alongside you every step of the way. He's in the race *with you*! He promises to give us strength when we're weary. The same power that brought him back from the grave lives *in us*. This power of the Holy Spirit is available every single step of our journey.

READY? Identify some motivational signs you've seen that stand out in your mind. What effect did they have on your physical race? What kind of motivation do you need right now in your life? Will you ask Jesus to fill you with the power you need?

GET SET. 2 Corinthians 12:9 "But he said to me, my grace is sufficient for you, for my power is made perfect in weakness. Therefore I will boast all the more gladly about my weaknesses, so that Christ's power may rest on me." (Also read Luke 8:43–48)

GO! *Lord Jesus, sometimes this journey gets rough. Help me soak up your power instead of seeking it from other sources. Thank you for the promise of your power when I am at my weakest moments. Amen.*

GOD'S TIMING

Proverbs 16:9 "In his heart a man plans his course, but the Lord determines his steps."

The day had finally arrived. Surrounded by thousands of runners, I inched my way to the start line. Excitement and adrenaline pumping through my body, I came face-to-face with my first full marathon.

Don't focus on your time. Don't focus on your pace. Just finish the race.

These words rang out loud in my mind. After a minor setback with a strained muscle, I accepted the fact that my goal was to simply finish the race. Period.

I found my unique rhythm: run for five minutes; walk for one. But after several miles, I found myself staring at the numbers on my watch. A huge relief washed over me when I approached the 13-mile marker. *I'm half way there!*

I then made a huge mistake. Obsessed with the numbers on my watch again, I began calculating. *Hmm, it's taken me two and a half hours to run half a marathon (which is about average for me!), so I should be able to finish this thing in about five hours if I double that. I'll even add an extra 30 minutes to compensate for a slower pace.*

In that moment I realistically figured I'd finish within five and a half hours. Seemed like a logical expectation, right? But I mistakenly fell for a trap. *I set up an expectation for something that was unknown.*

I plugged along through the next seven miles. Excitement flowing through every fiber of my body, I approached mile marker 20. This was a turning point. The most I'd run during training was 20. Venturing into unknown territory, I wondered if my body could make it past this point.

Yes! I breathed a sigh of relief passing mile 21. But then I looked at my watch again. *Okay, I'm taking longer according to my earlier calculations, but because I added that 30-minute buffer, I may still finish by five and a half hours.*

Passing mile 22, my left quad muscle wobbled. I slowed down. Then my right quad muscle quivered. Both legs jiggled like Jello!

At this point reality sunk in. I had to let go of my expectation for finishing in a certain time. Changing my pace altogether, I started walking slowly. After half a mile, I attempted to run. My quads started wobbling just after one minute! So this was my new pace. Run one minute; walk for five. Letting go of my expectation, I stopped focusing on my watch. God reminded me of my original goal: finish the race.

Turning the final corner, I inched my way across the finish line. It took me longer than I thought it would. But the numbers on my watch didn't matter. I'd finished the race!

How often do we make plans according to our own calculations? How often do we expect life to go a certain way, based upon what we've already experienced? Maybe we think we'll reach a specific goal in a short time, but later we realize it's taking much longer. Or we expect God to answer our prayers by a certain time.

We set ourselves up for disappointment when we expect things to happen in *our* timing. In *our* way. Peace would flow more freely in our lives if we trusted God's timing. God's ways are better than our ways. His timing is perfect. He is never late. Nothing takes him by surprise. He is ultimately in control of everything.

Wherever you are in your race of life, I encourage you to trust his timing. Trust his ways—one step at a time.

READY? Have you ever expected to finish a run in a certain time? Recall a time when an answered prayer came later than you expected. Were you able to see God's timing in that situation? Where in your life are you struggling to trust God's timing right now?

GET SET. Isaiah 55:8 "For my thoughts are not your thoughts, neither are my ways your ways, declares the Lord."

GO! *Dear Lord, I confess how I often want things to go according to my own plans. I lose focus of who you really are and think I'm in control. Forgive me for attempting to make things happen in my timing. Help me trust your timing, resting in the truth of who you are. Amen.*

HE KNOWS YOUR STATS

Psalm 139:3–4 "You discern my going out and my lying down; you are familiar with all my ways. Before a word is on my tongue you, Lord, know it completely."

In our ever-developing world of technology, various devices are available for tracking and recording our fitness stats. Garmin® watches track distance, pace, and exactly how many seconds, minutes, and hours have ticked by. (In my pre-Garmin® days, I drove my car around the block, using the odometer to figure out the distance I needed to run!)

Many have embraced the latest Fitbit® craze. A proud owner of one of these, I'm enthralled with this powerful tracking device. It monitors my daily steps, calorie consumption, flights climbed, heart rate, distance traveled, and how many hours I slept. I can even sync all these stats with my phone or laptop, analyzing in detail just how active—or inactive—I was on any given day. All of this information is displayed right at my fingertips.

To take it a step further, it blows me away that I'm not the only person Fitbit® tracks. I'm one of *thousands* of people—each with their own unique stats. How in the world can technology operate like this? How does it absorb all this information, keeping it specific for each and every person?

As impressive as our technology is with all its bells and whistles, there's something much more powerful than this. It's not a device. It's not something man has created.

God in all his infinite power and knowledge knows *everything* about each and every person in the whole wide world. Let that sink in for a moment. It's mind-boggling trying to wrap our human minds around this truth.

He knows the steps we've traveled (Proverbs 20:24), the number of hairs on our head (Luke 12:7), when we lie down, and our words before we speak them (Psalm 139:3–4).

In Matthew 10:29 Jesus tells us, "But not a single sparrow can fall to the ground without your Father knowing it." So if God notices all these birds, how much more does he know about us—people created in his own image?

Hebrews 4:13 says, "Nothing in all creation is hidden from God's sight. Everything is uncovered and laid bare before the eyes of him to whom we must give account."

It's one thing for him to know our spoken words, but according to Jeremiah 12:3, he examines the attitudes of our *heart*. Yikes! Even the stuff—good and bad—nobody else knows? Yes, he knows the stats of our soul. Let this bring comfort and not condemnation. He knows our fears and dreams. He understands our disappointments and desires. He comprehends our strengths and weaknesses. He even recognizes intimate things about us we don't understand ourselves. Now that's more complex than any manmade device that has been or ever will be developed!

If it's possible for the human mind to develop such powerful, complex technology, then how much more believable is it to grasp the fact that our sovereign God—the creator of the universe—is all-knowing and all-powerful?

But let's take it one step further. Not only does God know everything about us, but he loves us anyway. Our ugly messes are displayed before his eyes. But instead of condemning us, he syncs our sin-stained souls with the blood of Jesus, lavishing his forgiveness all over us.

READY? Take a moment and embrace the fact that God knows everything about your life. Is there an area of your life you've tried to hide from him? Reflect on today's scriptures and allow God's powerful presence to penetrate every area of your heart. The next time you charge your favorite device, let it be a reminder to you of God's power.

GET SET. Proverbs 5:21 "For a man's ways are in full view of the Lord, and he examines all his paths." (Also read Proverbs 20:24 and Luke 12:7)

GO! *Heavenly Father, my mind simply can't fathom your all-knowing, all-powerful presence. Help me accept by faith that you know every single detail of my life. May this truth comfort me when I doubt your involvement in my life. Amen.*

IN THE HEAT OF SUMMER

Isaiah 58:11 "The LORD will guide you always; he will satisfy your needs in a sun-scorched land and will strengthen your frame. You will be like a well-watered garden, like a spring whose waters never fail."

Heading out the door, you check the temperature. Already 80 degrees! Sweat begins pouring down your face. Just minutes into your run, you're already out of breath. The scorching sun feels like your enemy, staring you down. The humidity is unbearable—sapping all the energy from every fiber of your weary muscles. Your parched mouth craves water sooner than normal. Tempted to quit, you wonder if you can finish what you'd planned to run. You'd give anything to return to the previous months of cooler temps. But no, this is what it's like to run in the heat of summer.

Running in extreme heat puts more stress on the heart, and our muscles don't get as much oxygen. The higher the humidity level, the harder it is for our bodies to evaporate sweat, making it difficult to cool down. No wonder we reach exhaustion sooner!

But runners who want to maintain fitness goals and train for fall races have no choice but to run in the heat. (If you live where it's hot all year-round, my heart goes out to you!) So instead of quitting, we *must* adapt to the heat. There are multiple tips on beating the heat, but the most essential thing we can do is maintain optimal hydration. We have to drink *more* than what we're used to—even when we don't *feel* thirsty. Without enough water we risk dehydration, causing muscle cramps, dizziness, and nausea. It's a matter of survival.

Just as runners hydrate more frequently in extreme heat, Christ followers must run to the source of our living water—especially when we're trudging through a desert season of life. Ever been there? Before the day even starts, waves of exhaustion wash over you. You dread the day ahead. *Can't I just pull the covers over my head and go back to sleep?* You've lost your joy. Your motivation to live purposefully has disappeared. Your faith feels like it's dried up, leaving your soul parched. Maybe you don't feel God near you. Perhaps you've given up waiting for an answer to your prayer. Every fiber of your weary soul is burdened. Worn out from stress and anxiety, you wonder if you'll ever make it to the other side of the desert you're crawling through. *Why even bother? Does it really matter?*

Dear friend, it *does* matter! Although Jesus told us to expect trials in this fallen world, he promised to never leave us—even when we don't *feel* it (John 16:33). Desert seasons often usher in waves of exhaustion, fear, and hopelessness—crashing in and pushing out our peace and joy. But instead of quitting, we must resolve to stay faithful, embracing Jesus with our whole heart. Even if our soul doesn't *feel* thirsty, we must fix our eyes on him and cling to him more than ever before. Spending time in prayer. Soaking up promises from his word. Resting in his presence. Reaching out to him desperately. Without him, we risk falling into hopelessness and despair. It's a matter of survival!

I don't know how long your desert season may last. But I can promise you that Jesus is with you every step of the way. Your sun-scorched soul will be watered ... by him alone. The heavy burdens weighing you down will be lifted ... by him alone. The empty places of your heart will be filled ... by him alone.

READY? If you're walking through a desert season, what are you actively doing to maintain your relationship with Jesus? Recall a previous time in your life when you walked through a desert season. What insight did you gain from that time in your life? Claim a promise from God's word you can cling to in times you may not feel his presence.

GET SET. John 4:14 "But those who drink the water I give will never be thirsty again. It becomes a fresh, bubbling spring within them, giving them eternal life."

GO! *Jesus, I praise your name for your faithfulness to me. Even when I'm going through a rough time, I thank you for your promises. Help me embrace your presence when I'm walking through a desert. May your truth fill my thirst and satisfy my longings. You truly are the living water. Amen.*

WHO'S BEHIND YOU?

2 Corinthians 1:3-4 "Praise be to the God and Father of our Lord Jesus Christ, the father of compassion and the God of all comfort, who comforts us in all our troubles so that we can comfort those in any trouble with the comfort we ourselves receive from God."

Panting to catch my breath, I shuffled to a halt. Wiping sweat off my brow and looking at my watch, I felt a twinge of disappointment wash over me. My pace was slower than normal for our group's weekly long run. Walking toward my car, I heard an unfamiliar voice. *"Hey! Wait up!"* Turning around, a woman approached me, a smile on her face. *"I was following you the whole time; you've got a pretty consistent pace."* Huh? Someone was following me? *"I'm training for my first half-marathon. I'm excited and nervous at the same time."* After introductions, we struck up a conversation and I gave her some tips for training. With five half-marathons under my belt, I felt confident in guiding my new friend on her unfamiliar journey.

No matter what your pace is, there's always going to be someone running behind you. Brand-new runners venturing out for the very first time. Runners lacking confidence. Runners who don't know what's up ahead. Runners who are watching your every move to see how you're running *your* race. These runners are in the same spot you *used to be*. Yes, there is someone always running behind you whether you notice them or not.

In our race of faith, there is someone running behind you, dear friend. Sometimes we can get so caught up in the pace of our own race that we forget to stop and turn around to help those who are running behind us. There are people watching us whether we realize it or not. People who are new Christians just starting out. People who are stuck in a rut and need some encouragement. People walking a path you've already navigated through. But do we ever slow down our precalculated pace long enough to help someone else? Do we slow down long enough to walk alongside someone who is hurting?

Often we may think our pain and suffering is in vain. As genuine followers of Christ, we can testify that God carries us with strength and pours his comfort on us during hard times. He does a work *in* us during these seasons. But it doesn't stop there! He longs to do something *through* us. He desires for us to embrace those behind us and point them to him. To lovingly comfort them. To assure them they're going to make it. This is what the body of Christ is called to do.

So who's behind you? If you have children, they are watching you whether you realize it or not. What about that young mom with multiple children? You might be an empty-nester who could encourage her with your insight and wisdom. Is there someone at work or in your neighborhood struggling through a season of life you've already traveled through? I promise you that you won't have to look very long. There will always be someone beginning to crawl onto a path you've just finished running. Ask God to show you. And don't be surprised when they soak up your encouragement like a breath of fresh air.

READY? Do you find yourself too preoccupied with your own pace in life? Genuinely pray and ask God to show you who's behind you at this season of life. What is the next step you can take to pour into that person? If you're feeling anxious, ask God for his peace.

GET SET. Romans 15:1 "We who are strong in faith should help the weak with their weaknesses, and not please only ourselves."

GO! *Heavenly Father, thank you for the reminder of past times when you've comforted me through difficult seasons. I praise you for giving me strength. Show me the people you want me to pour into. Give me courage and wisdom. I long to point others to the power you've given me. Amen.*

THE WHOLE BODY

1 Corinthians 12:27 "Now you are the body of Christ, and each one of you is a part of it."

The human body is a remarkable creation. It's amazing how our bodies are designed with the capacity to run. Every single part plays a crucial role—working together—propelling the body forward. But if even *one part* malfunctions, it affects the entire body. Even the seemingly insignificant parts need attention for the whole body to operate at 100 percent.

The larger muscles of our feet generate most of the motion needed for pounding the pavement. But the smaller muscles *within* the foot keep us stable, supporting the arch. If these smaller muscles are weakened, it can lead to plantar fasciitis, a painful condition affecting one's ability to run efficiently.[11]

Our leg muscles go through a large range of motion, working from top to bottom. The quadriceps, hamstrings, and calf muscles each perform their specific duties, giving stability and support. But if you strain, pull, or tear any of these muscles, your whole body feels the pain.

Hip strength is imperative for any runner. Our hip flexors facilitate upward leg movement, stabilizing our body as we run.

But that stability suddenly collapses when an inflamed tendon or stress fracture shows up.

Your arms might not seem like a priority when running, yet they help with balance, momentum, and speed. Shoulder pain in your arm slows you down. A pinched nerve disrupts your balance, quickly leaving you disabled.

Just as each body part works together for one purpose, the body of Christ (the Church) works the same way. When we choose to follow Christ, we're given spiritual gifts (Romans 12:4—8). These gifts equip us to serve others within the church. When we all use these to our full potential, the body of Christ thrives and functions as it was designed by God. But when one part is weakened, the rest of the body is affected.

Some people are leaders and teachers. They're in the spotlight, getting much attention. But behind the scenes you might not notice the other people supporting *them*. Some are praying and encouraging them. Others attend to the details so the leaders can focus on the big picture. Not everyone plays the role of a foot or leg. You might be a tiny muscle nobody even knows about, but without you the others can't function. When you're weakened, it disables those around you.

Your role might be supporting others through your hospitality or finances. Or maybe you're the one called to preach, lead, or teach in some capacity. Regardless of what your gift is, we're all connected to each other, like the intertwined tendons, ligaments, and muscles of the body. There are no insignificant ministries within the church. Jesus is the head of them all. He's the one holding us together, propelling us forward.

Even if you're thriving in your specific role, there are times when others lose their momentum. They collapse from unexpected turmoil. The fibers of their heart are torn in pain. Instead of running their race full force, they come to a screeching halt. In those moments, each member of the body of Christ is called to slow down and attend to their injuries—equipping them to get back on course.

READY? Recall a time when you experienced an injury. How did it affect the rest of your body? Can you identify your role within the church? If so, are you actively using your gifts and talents for God's kingdom? If not, are you willing to discover what they are and seek a place to serve within the church?

GET SET. Ephesians 4:16 "From him the whole body, joined and held together by every supporting ligament, grows and builds itself up in love, as each part does its work." (Also read 1 Corinthians 12:12–26)

GO! *Dear Jesus, give me wisdom to see what my part is within your body. Equip me and prepare me for what you've called me to do. Show me how to serve others and love them. When others in the church are hurting, please make me sensitive to their needs. Amen.*

NEVER SAY NEVER!

Deuteronomy 31:6 "Be strong and courageous. Do not be afraid or terrified because of them, for the LORD your God goes with you; he will never leave you nor forsake you."

The first time I ran a half marathon, I found myself laughing at a certain point in the race. When runners approached mile marker number nine, something drastic happened. Up until this point, everyone—half-marathoners and full-marathoners— was running on the same course together. Everyone was mixed in and you didn't know who was running which race. But then at mile marker number nine, the course divided. It split down the middle. The half-marathoners turned left and the full-marathoners turned right. This is where I found myself laughing out loud and thinking very clear:

There is no way I'd ever run a full marathon! I could NEVER do that! Heck, I don't even know if I'll finish **this** *race. Those people are crazy! I don't understand why or how they do it.*

Fast forward four years and six half marathons later, I'd registered for a *full* marathon after a stirring in my heart. It was time for a new challenge. Before I knew it, I stood at the start line of my first marathon.

Approaching mile marker number nine, I'd reached the crucial turning point where the race split. The bright orange warning signs flashed in front of me. A man blasted through a megaphone, "Attention runners! Half-marathoners go left! Marathoners go right!" Runners chaotically dashed from one side to the other. Two runners brushed up against me, merging left. And then the truth hit me hard: I was now running on the *right* side of the road—with *fewer* people. I glanced over my left shoulder, watching the half-marathoners fade out of my sight. Only four more miles and they'd cross their finish line, but for me, I had seventeen more to go. After the initial rush of excitement wore off, the reality of my situation sunk in. I was traveling on a path I previously said I'd *never* take. Here I was—attempting something I said I'd NEVER do!

How many times in our lives have we dug our feet in the sand exclaiming similar words—*I will never go there. I could never walk that path. I'd never survive a trial like that*—but then later you find yourself walking that forbidden path, the one you said you'd never step onto. Maybe God has called you into a season of life you never dreamed you'd find yourself. Or maybe there's an area of your life you're clinging too tightly to, refusing to let go. Perhaps you're gripped with grief or fear because of an unexpected trial.

I've heard people utter these words over the years: *I'll never be able to lose weight; it's just too hard. I will never homeschool, I don't have the patience for that. I could never leave my hometown, I've lived here my whole life. I could never invite my neighbor to church, I couldn't handle the rejection. I could never adopt, I'm fine with the family I have.*

I could never _____? Fill in the blank. What is it for you?

It's possible that your *I could never* is fear lurking in the deepest part of your heart. Maybe your *I could never* is something God is nudging you towards, requiring a deeper trust. Whatever it is, God promises to be with us through it all. Let me remind you of a truth where God uses the word *never*. To those who put their faith in Jesus, he promises to *never* leave us or forsake us (Hebrews 13:5). Instead of clinging to your *I could never*, embrace the truth of his promise *to never leave you.*

READY? Have you ever done something after you said you'd never do it? What caused you to step out and change your mind? Identify an area of your life you're saying *never* to right now. Ask God to clarify whether it's fear speaking or his gentle nudge.

GET SET. Hebrews 13:5 "Be content with what you have because God has said, 'Never will I leave you. Never will I forsake you.'"

GO! *Heavenly Father, help me trust you when my flesh says "Never!" When I'm gripped with fear, help me step out in faith. Help me let go of worry about future trials, resting in assurance that you'll be with me when those times come. Thank you for the promise of never leaving me! Amen.*

WHEN YOUR BODY
WEARS DOWN

2 Corinthians 4:16 "Therefore, we do not lose heart. Though outwardly we are wasting away, yet inwardly we are being renewed day by day."

She loved running. This passion fueled her for many years. But one day the excruciating pain in her knees and hips drove her to see her doctor. After waiting for x-ray results, the dreaded diagnosis hit her smack in the face. "I hate to tell you this, but you have osteoarthritis," the doctor informed. Losing heart, she dropped her head in despair.

Osteoarthritis. Not something any runner wants to hear. Also known as a degenerative joint disease, it causes inflammation and pain in one or more joints. A lifetime of walking, exercising, and moving around in general takes a toll on our cartilage. Once arthritis of this type sets in, the cartilage deteriorates, which can lead to bone scraping against bone.[12] Even if you don't develop osteoarthritis, the stark truth remains: we lose muscle tone and bone strength the older we get.

Dear friend, don't let this truth bring you down. It's an uncontrollable fact that our physical bodies will wear down. They won't last forever. Even the bodies of the most elite runners will eventually wear out. Living in a fallen world, all human beings have a common condition. It's called *sin*. But as followers of Christ, we don't have to lose heart—dropping our heads in despair. We can rejoice! Why? Our soul doesn't waste away. Our soul is renewed day by day. We become more like Christ through the process of sanctification. The more we seek after him, the stronger our faith becomes. The more we rest in his presence, the power of sin loses its grip on us. The more we humbly surrender to his calling, the more he increases in us.

And the good news gets even better. Even after our physical bodies wear out and we take our last breath on this earth, we are immediately ushered into the presence of God. We'll see him face-to-face. He promises us a brand-new resurrection body. A body that won't wear out. A body that won't deteriorate. A body without any pain. Who knows, maybe we'll even get to continue our running journey in heaven. No shin splints. No cramping muscles. No torn ligaments. No aching knees. Can you imagine that?

So until that day comes, we keep on running. We keep pressing on. We run our hearts out until we can't take another step. No matter what type of physical diagnosis we receive for our earthly body, we'll graciously accept it when that time comes. In the meantime, we keep running in our spiritual race. We keep pressing into Jesus. We rejoice in the fact that we've already received our spiritual diagnosis. We are sinners saved by grace.

READY? Is your life currently affected by any physical pain? What are you most looking forward to when you will experience living in a brand-new body in heaven? Whether you have physical pain or not, is your faith growing stronger? What steps do you need to take to keep God the center of your life?

GET SET. 1 Timothy 4:8 "For while bodily training is of some value, godliness is of value in every way, as it holds promise for the present life and also for the life to come."

GO! *Lord Jesus, I feel weary sometimes living in this physical body! Help me not to focus solely on my physical condition, but to care for my soul. Thank you for the promise of a new body in heaven. But even more so, thank you for the promise of seeing you face-to-face one day. Help me live in such a way that my life pleases you for the days I run my race of faith on this earth. Amen.*

THE CROWD AT THE FINISH LINE

Hebrews 12:1 "Therefore, since we are surrounded by such a great cloud of witnesses, let us throw off everything that hinders and the sin that so easily entangles, and let us run with perseverance the race marked out for us."

Running on empty, the race had completely drained me. Sweat pouring down my face, I wondered if I'd made a mistake. Maybe I wasn't cut out to run this race. I'd trained properly, yet it sure didn't feel that way now. The motivation I had in the beginning slowly diminished with each mile of the race. Did it really matter if I finished? Would anyone even notice?

The last leg of the race was ahead, just around the corner. Boisterous shouts erupted in the air. Shrieking whistles pierced my ears. Thunderous clapping ushered us along in jubilant applause. All of a sudden I felt rejuvenated! A sense of accomplishment welled up inside. The hard work *was* worth the excitement that washed over me. The crowd surrounded me on both sides as I crossed the finish line. Yes! I'd finally made it!

In Hebrews 12, we're told about a cloud of witnesses that surrounds us. Although they aren't visible to us, they are ever present in the *spiritual* realm. In Hebrews 11,—often called the hall of faith—we read about these heroes of the past, examples who inspire us today. Those who believed and hoped, even though they didn't get to see Jesus before they died. The Greek meaning for the word witnesses is *testifiers*. Each one mentioned in the passage bears testimony to the power of God's faithfulness. God used them to lay the foundation we stand on today. They persevered until the very end. They ran their races well and were ushered into the presence of God, their redemption complete.

Imagine Abraham, Jacob, and Isaac, the patriarchs of our faith, cheering us on! Imagine Moses and Joshua urging us to stay strong and courageous on our journey of faith. What about Joseph? Think of all the turmoil he endured, yet he stayed focused on God's promises. Can you envision him walking on the sideline of your race giving you a high five? What would he say? *Hang in there! Don't stop. Keep going. Your pain will be worth it when you reach the finish line.* Then there's Rahab, a runner we'd never expect to be mentioned in this race of faith. Some might say she wasn't even worthy to sign up for the race to begin with. But her name in the hall of faith bears testimony to the boundless grace of God. The kind of grace that redeems—restoring surrendered sinners to him. What would she say if she could see us struggling in our race? *You can do it. Lean on him. You're going to make it!*

Just as we grow weary along a difficult race course, it's easy to lose our motivation in life. We start out with such powerful zeal. We think nothing could ever stop us, but then something happens, slowing us down. Our excitement fizzles and we lose our focus. We wonder what our purpose really is. Does our life matter? Yes, it does matter!

Others have crossed the finish line before us. They have persevered and fought the good fight of faith. One day when we cross the heavenly finish line, the hall of faith heroes will give us high fives! Although from different generations, our common thread will be that Jesus enabled us to persevere … one step at a time.

READY? Identify an area of your life where you've lost motivation or feel a lack of purpose. What do you need to get back on track? What does your temporary setback look like through the lens of eternity? If you have loved ones in heaven, imagine them cheering you on.

GET SET. Hebrews 3:14 "For if we are faithful to the end, trusting God just as firmly as when we first believed, we shall share in all that belongs to Christ." (Also read Hebrews 11:4–40)

GO! *Dear God, I confess that many times I feel weary and want to quit. I lose my motivation. My purpose isn't clear. Please help me regain clarity and keep going. Help me remember those who have gone before me. May their inspiration and example be a reminder that just as you were with them, you are with me now. Amen.*

THE PRIZE

1 Corinthians 9:24–25 "Don't you realize that in a race everyone runs, but only one person gets the prize? So run to win! All athletes are disciplined in their training. They do it to win a prize that will fade away, but we do it for an eternal prize."

Elite runners compete for more than shiny medals. They're out to claim cash prizes. Lelisa Desisa and Caroline Rotich each claimed $150,000 in prize money as the first man and woman crossing the finish line in the 2015 Boston marathon.[13] Winners of the New York and Chicago marathons receive $100,000. Topping the men's and women's list for most lucrative lifetime prize money winners are Haile Gebreselasie and Paula Radcliffe[14]. We're talking seven-figure amounts here! For these runners, it's more than a onetime cash prize. It's their livelihood.

Most runners aren't competing for cash prizes in the elite category. The next best thing might be claiming a trophy, ribbon, or plaque for the top three spots in each age category. But realistically, these prizes are handed out to a small percentage of runners.

For the average runner, what's the prize? Another medal to hang on the wall? A goodie bag of coupons and samples? How about a race tee-shirt? Some say the prize is the accomplishment of *finishing the race*. Nothing tangible. Just the inward satisfaction from crossing the finish line.

In 2 Timothy 4, the apostle Paul writes about a race. In his time, the most prestigious event in Olympia was the footrace. Athletes trained for months, preparing for this ultimate event. A wreath of wild olive was placed atop the winner's head. Winning runners were also given the privilege of building statues of themselves inside the town sanctuary.[15] Although Paul mentions a physical race, his underlying message is about a different kind of race.

Whether we ever lace up running shoes or not, we're all running a race. He's talking about the race of living the Christian life here on earth. He urges us as Christ followers to embrace our faith and run in such a way as to win an *eternal* prize, an imperishable crown.

Things on this earth are perishable. Olive wreaths wilt away. Cash prizes are spent. Medals collect dust and eventually rust. The fame of winning the most prestigious races fades away as time goes on.

We don't know how many days we have in this life on earth, but one thing is for certain: if we are true followers of Christ, we will enter into heaven one day and see him face-to-face. On that day, no amount of money will be handed to us. No medal will be hung around our neck. And there certainly won't be any statue-building ceremony. No, dear friend, our prize will be greater than anything we've ever gained on this earth. It will be the joy of seeing our savior. The glory of his presence for eternity. To hear Jesus say, "Well done, good and faithful servant," will be far greater than any earthly prize we've ever claimed. This imperishable crown of life won't fade, wilt, or rust away.

It's okay for us to run our best. For some of us, that best may lead to prizes. There's nothing wrong with that! But don't ever ignore the big picture. Don't forget that you're running a lifelong race of faith, leading to something imperishable. The next time you earn a medal, ribbon, or trophy, may it remind you to stay focused on your eternal prize in heaven.

READY? What motivates you to run? If you've gained some tangible prize like a medal, how did it make you feel when it was placed around your neck? When you're going through a slump in your spiritual walk, can you let today's scripture be a reminder of what awaits you in heaven?

GET SET. 2 Timothy 4:7–8 "I have fought the good fight, I have finished the race, I have kept the faith. Finally, there is laid up for me the crown of righteousness, which the Lord, the righteous judge, will give to me on that day, and not to me only but also to all who have loved his appearing."

GO! *Lord Jesus, help me stay focused on what really matters. Help me see life through an eternal lens. Thank you for the promise of seeing you face-to-face one day. Until then, may I embrace my race all the days you give me here on earth. Amen.*

ENDNOTES

1. "Common Causes of Injuries" (http://www.jeffgalloway.com)

2. "Quotes about Running Hills"
   https://www.verywell.com/quotes-about-running-hills-2911765

3. "AZ quotes," Eamonn Coghlan Quotes,
   http://www.azquotes.com/author/44892-Eamonn_Coghlan

4. *The Guardian*, "Does Music Help You to Run Faster?"
   Adharanand Finn,
   http://www.theguardian.com/lifeandstyle/2012/apr/22/
   does-music-help-you-run-faster

5. *BBC News*, "Health, How Music Can Aid Athletic
   Performance," http://www.bbc.com/news/health-10767128

6. "Against the Wall," Nancy Averett, http://www.runnersworld.com/running-tips/ how-to-avoid-hitting-the-wall-while-running

7. "How 'Perception of Effort' Can Make or Break a Race," Matt Fitzgerald, http://running.competitor.com/2015/10/training/ how-perception-of-effort-can-make-or-break-a-race_137729

8. Running Times Archives, "Rosie Ruiz Tries to Steal the Boston Marathon," http://www.runnersworld.com/running-times-info/ rosie-ruiz-tries-to-steal-the-boston-marathon

9. "In a 26-Mile Slog, a Shortcut Can Be Tempting," Andrew W. Lehren, http://www.nytimes.com/2009/11/01/ sports/01runners.html

10. "Spotlight on Highway Safety," Dr. Allan Williams, http://www.ghsa.org/html/files/pubs/spotlights/ spotlightped2014.pdf

11. "Runner's World, Plantar Fasciitis," http://www.runnersworld.com/tag/plantar-fasciitis

12. "What Do You Want to Know About Osteoarthritis?" David Heitz, http://www.healthline.com/health/osteoarthritis

13. "Lelisa Desisa, Carolyn Rotich Win Titles at 119th Boston Marathon," http://espn.go.com/boston/story/_/ id/12727515/119th-boston-marathon-lelisa-desisa-caroline-rotich-win-titles

14. "Races and Places," Allison Wade and Dan Fuehrer, http://www.runnersworld.com/run-the-numbers/runnings-most-lucrative-road-races-biggest-earners

15. http://www.olympia-greece.org/contests.html